John Samuel Fay was born in Brazil and brought up in New Zealand until the age of nine when he came to England. From school in 1940, he joined the Fleet Air Arm as a pilot and spent two years in HMS Victorious. After some months in the Service Trials Unit, he was appointed, in 1944, to the first helicopter course in the country. After the war, he joined the BEA Helicopter Unit subsequently becoming a Test Pilot with Westland Aircraft. He is keen on ballroom and sequence dancing, photography, gardening and music.

FIRST NAMES AS
LIMERICKS

FIRST NAMES AS LIMERICKS

John Samuel Fay

ATHENA PRESS
LONDON

FIRST NAMES AS LIMERICKS
Copyright © John Samuel Fay 2004

ISBN 1 84401 378 2

First Published 2004 by
ATHENA PRESS
Queen's House, 2 Holly Road
Twickenham TW1 4EG
United Kingdom

Printed for Athena Press

To Dorothy

PREFACE

When I started writing this book I became increasingly amazed at the number of names in use by the English-speaking peoples. Unfortunately it is not possible to include verses for every name and, indeed, the contents are only a selection of the 2100 verses I originally wrote. I am sorry if the name you seek is not here.

My friends and relations who read this book may rest assured that the contents do not apply to them. Everyone has a name and my verses are composed using words to rhyme with that name. I occasionally mention some well-known people (such as Dwight), but the content of the limericks are usually invented, using the rhymes that are the most fitting.

My main criterion regarding the verses is that the name must appear at the end of the first line. I could have done otherwise to make matters easier for myself, especially where the number of rhymes available was limited and I had to use two or more words to match the name. Because of my self-imposed limitation the content of the verse often had to be even more zany than usual, and the overall quality has considerable variation.

Although limericks tend to be bawdy, I wanted to reach as wide a readership as possible so I have used material that is suitable for people of all ages.

As regards the metre, whilst keeping to the usual format where possible, my rule of thumb has been that if one can fit the words into the tune I used in my childhood then it is all right. I am comforted by the fact even that the following old favourite can be sung:

> There was a young man from Japan
> Who wrote verses that never would scan.
> When his friends told him so
> He replied, "Yes I know
> But I like to get as many words in the last line as I jolly well possibly can."

In my past publications, usually of an aeronautical nature, I have used my name, John Fay. John Fays in the aviation business must be fairly rare, but in the wider world there are hundreds of us so I have used my full name, John Samuel Fay, to avoid confusion as to which of us is writing. Indeed, while working on this book I found another John Fay who had had limericks published!

I made considerable use of Rosalind Fergusson's *The Penguin Rhyming Dictionary* and also of my ancient copy of J Walker's *The Rhyming Dictionary of the English Language*, the latter being originally produced long before the advent of computers. Since the words are in alphabetical order in accordance with the reversed spelling of the words the original work must have taken many years to write, and I offer my humble tribute to a long-dead man. I thank both these authors without whom my task would have been infinitely greater.

I must also thank Adrian Room, the author of *A Name For Your Baby*, and Hilary Pence, the author of *The Complete Book Of Baby Names Traditional And Modern*. I could not have written this book without using their works as a main source of information.

My thanks also to my wife, Dorothy, who has been a great source of encouragement to me and has ably assisted by reading through and correcting my many mistakes. She has been valuable also in occasionally giving me an appropriate word or phrase when my brain has gone into neutral.

A

A balding young man called Aaron...

AARON

A balding young man called Aaron
Was thought to be a bit of a queer 'un.
He said his new wig
Was much too big
And wanted dark brown, not a fair 'un.

ABBEY (ALSO ABBIE AND ABBY)

There once was a sweetie called Abbey
Who was neither too tall nor too baggy.
I asked, "Are you well?"
She said, "I can't smell,
I've a cold in by doze, bud I'm habby."

ABEL

There was a young brother called Abel
Who was renowned in a biblical fable.
He didn't last long
For Cain did him wrong
For he, we all know, was unstable.

ABRAHAM

A bright young man – Abraham,
Could draw a neat diagram.
He could split the atom
And play football for Chatham
But he couldn't open my tin of ham.

ABRAM

A strange old man called Abram
Used to drive around town in a pram.
His motive force
Was Worcestershire sauce
Mixed up with strawberry jam.

ABSALOM

We knew a young man – Absalom,
Who skied down a difficult slalom.
He was much too stiff
And went over a cliff;
The last word we heard was "shalom!"

ADA

A pretty young girl called Ada
Got caught by a piratical raider.
She thought it was funny
When he offered her money
But she did what he wished when he paid her.

ADAM

Said a short-sighted man called Adam,
"I got stuck in some wet tarmadadam.
I'd quite lost my way;
It's ruined my whole day,
And as for my shoes – I've had 'em."

ADDI (ALSO ADDY)

An enthusiastic golfer called Addi
Was the nightmare of every caddy.
His friends said that he would
Make Donald the Dub look good.
But the pro said, "Och, they're just faddy."

ADELA

A girl with a kayak called Adela
Was known as an expert paddler.
As a horsewoman she would
Have been really quite good,
But her steeds always tried to unsaddle her.

ADELAIDE

There was a young cook called Adelaide
Who added some deadly nightshade.
But business declined
When her clientele dined
And the poor girl never got paid.

ADELE

There was a young dancer called Adele
Who was learning a step when she fell.
Her partner said, "Bother!
Why did you not hover?
If you had we'd be getting on well."

ADELINE

A university student – Adeline,
Worked hard for a degree in Strine.[1]
She learnt to say, "Hi,
What a lovely dye,
But I'm afraid it'll come on to ryne."

ADRIAN

In old times a surveyor called Adrian
Would not use a *degree* but a *radian*.
He caused confusion to all
When he started to build the wall,
So he resigned in favour of Hadrian.

AGATHA

An explosives expert called Agatha
Was known to all as a blatherer.
She tackled a live bomb
With too much aplomb,
And they used brush and pan to gather her.

---

[1] Strine: the alleged Australian language.

AIDEN

There was a young postman called Aiden
Who walked down the street heavy-laden.
In very thick fog
He trod on a frog
Which turned into a beautiful maiden.

AILEEN

There was a young student called Aileen
Whose maths were the worst that I've seen.
She coloured the angles
Of all her triangles,
And her best was a purple scalene.

AILSA

A hypochondriac girl called Ailsa
Invariably tells me what ails her.
She works in a bar
So it's better by far
When she says to me, "Your ale, sir!"

AL

A monarchist man called Al
Once got on his bike with a pal.
They reached Buck House
By following a mouse
And a golden coach right up The Mall.

ALAN

There was an old man named Alan
Who lived on the Isle of Arran.
They said he was thoughtless
To live in a fortress,
And called him the bold bad baron.

ALASDAIR (ALSO ALISDAIR)

A young politician – Alasdair,
Was plumbing the depths of despair.
The natives were rioting
Which he found quite disquieting
For he'd just been made Chargé d'Affaires.

ALBERT

Said a dying old sergeant called Albert,
"To me you've been such a pal, Bert;
As a memento of battles
I'll leave you my chattels
And also my favourite halbert."[2]

ALBERTA

There was a young linguist – Alberta
Who she said that nothing could hurt her.
They proved her wrong
When she went to Hong Kong,
And was made to translate some Goethe.

ALDIS

A lonely old man named Aldis
Said, "I'm getting away from all this."
When they asked him why
He said, "I'm going to try
To find bliss with an unmarried Swiss."

ALDOUS (ALSO ALDUS)

There was a young student called Aldous
Whose *operandi* was really quite *modus*.
It's terribly sad
That his Latin was bad
But 'twas his English that really bored us.

---

[2] Halbert: an ancient axe-like weapon which denoted the rank of sergeant.

ALDRED

There was a young tripper – Aldred
Who went for a tour round the Med.
And just for a lark
He swam with a shark,
But you can't swim far when you're dead.

ALDUS. SEE ALDOUS.

ALDWIN

An aspiring young man named Aldwin
Said his father knew Stanley Baldwin.
But they didn't agree,
(Dad was Labour, you see),
Much to his regret and chagrin.

ALEC

There was a young author called Alec
Who wrote all his words in italic.
He said that the stress
Would always impress
And people would think him angelic.

ALEX

There was a strange man called Alex
Whose make-up was ever so complex.
They say that for fun
He'd eat half a bun
Then climb up a holm-oak (or ilex).

ALEXANDER

There once was a King Alexander
Who issued warlike memoranda.
It was by his exertions
That he conquered the Persians
Thus raising to rare heights their dander.

ALEXANDRA

A flighty young girl – Alexandra,
Paid a very quick call on Cassandra.
That seer was curt:
"Just lengthen your skirt
Or you'll become a little philanderer."

ALEXANDRINA

There was once an Alexandrina
Who was destined to be a Tsarina.
But on seeing the Tsar
She took off in her car
And it's years since anyone's seen her.

ALF

A precise young man called Alf
Never did things by half.
And if there's a rhyme
Please spend some time
And write lines on his behalf.

ALFIE

There was an old man called Alfie,
Who never would pay us our fee.
If they find his body
In a dried-up wadi,
Please don't tell the cops about me.

ALFONSO (ALSO ALPHONSO)

A hen-pecked man called Alfonso,
Had a wife who said, "You do go on so,
Why don't you stop talking
And for once try walking
And go out with our poor old Bonzo."

ALFRED

A colour-blind man called Alfred
Once painted his house half-red.
The rest – and it's true –
Was a deep shade of blue.
When I saw it I nearly dropped dead.

ALGIE (ALSO ALGY)

There was a young man called Algie
Who suffered from bad odontalgy.
He told his supervisor,
"It's my left incisor,
And look at my face, it's so bulgy."

ALI

A budding young actor called Ali
Travelled west from the island of Bali.
When he reached Djakarta
He ate a chipolata
Which proved to be his finale.

ALICE

An aristocratic old girl called Alice
Was invited to Buckingham Palace.
There she ate gammon
And a little smoked salmon
And drank wine from a golden chalice.

ALISDAIR. SEE ALASDAIR.

ALISON

A very tall girl called Alison
Was well known to the local garrison.
They proposed by the score
Until she said, "No more!
You're all much too small by comparison."

ALISTAIR

A very young joiner – Alistair,
Used bits of wood for a chair.
Said brother Humphrey,
"It's not too comfy,
I'd prefer it to be stuffed with hair."

ALLAN (ALSO ALLEN)

A young explorer called Allan
Had an attitude most crocodilian.
He'd lie in the mud
Just chewing the cud
And drinking up slime by the gallon.

ALLIE (ALSO ALLY)

There was a dotty lady called Allie
With whom I became quite pally.
She'd repeat many stories
About her past glories,
But I fear that they seldom did tally.

ALMEDA

There was a new student called Almeda
Who decided to study some lieder.
When they said, "Can you sing?"
She replied, "Not a thing,
But I once went to see Aïda."

ALOYS (ALSO LOYS)

There was an Irish girl called Aloys
Who used to play with her toys.
She became a colleen[3]
At the age of fourteen,
At which time she discovered – boys!

---

[3] Colleen: (Irish) a girl.

ALOYSIUS

There was an official named Aloysius
Whose character was quite malicious.
So he changed his name
And then became
Well-liked and quite auspicious.

ALPHONSO. SEE ALFONSO.

AMABEL

There was an old girl – Amabel,
Whose voice was like… I won't tell.
But the size of her girth
Caused a great deal of mirth
For she resembled a ten-ton bell.

AMADEUS

I once knew a violinist called Amadeus
And listened to him 'cos he made us.
But we disliked the fiddle
So would escape in the middle.
We wouldn't do that if he'd paid us.

AMANDA

A lazy young girl called Amanda
Used to sit all day on her veranda.
When they said, "You're a slut
And in a bit of a rut."
She sued the whole lot for slander.

AMBER

An African dancer called Amber
Was expert at doing the samba.
Her left whisk was bold
And a joy to behold
But brilliant when she stepped on a mamba.

AMBROSE

There was an old author – Ambrose,
Who sat all day writing ham prose.
In fact some might say
"He's just like John Fay."
But if so you're one of my foes!

AMELIA

A green-fingered girl called Amelia
Once grew an enormous camellia
When the neighbours did glower,
She said to this flower,
"Now I've got to conceal yer."

AMIE (ALSO AMY)

There was a young pilot called Amie
Who said, "This life is so samey,
I'll fly to Westphalia
Or perhaps to Australia.
And when I've done it they'll acclaim me."

AMOS

A young businessman – Amos,
Used to run his own firm at a loss.
It wasn't the VAT
Which made him do that
But his failure to act as a boss.

AMY. SEE AMIE.

AMYAS

There was a young chump called Amyas
Who thought to himself, "I'm an ass.
The mnemonics I remember
Are forgotten by November,
If only I weren't so crass."

ANASTASIA

A Russian Grand Duchess – Anastasia
Went out of her way to amaze yer.
She claimed, "This daughter
Just missed the slaughter."
But about facts she was somewhat hazier.

ANDREA

There once was a farm girl called Andrea
Whose piglets she liked to hand rear.
There were odd features
About her other creatures –
There was a llama, a kiwi and rhea.

ANDREW

A budding young lawyer called Andrew
Learnt to make wills and sue.
But when in court
He was pulled up short
When his logic became all askew.

ANGELICA

There was a young fighter – Angelica,
Who was so good no girl could lick her.
Her favourite ploy
Was to shout, "Ship ahoy!"
When her opponent looked round she'd kick her.

ANGELINA

There is an old ghost – Angelina,
So wraith-like that no one has seen her.
So how do you suppose
That anyone knows
She was once a famous Tsarina.

ANGHARAD

There was an odd girl – Angharad,
Who was feeling full up and haggard.
For her strange eccentricity
Of dabbling with electricity
Gave her a capacitance of one farad.[4]

ANGUS

The following limerick should be read with a Birmingham accent.

A young airport driver called Angus
Towed an aircraft away to the hangers.
The pilot called, "Stop,
You stupid young clot
I'm just flying off with some bangers."

ANITA

A very fast runner – Anita,
Once had a race with a cheetah.
After some confusion
There was just one conclusion;
And that cat proceeded to eat her.

ANN (ALSO ANNE)

A time-travelling genius called Ann
Went off to the casino in Cannes.
And just for a bet
She attempted roulette
And finished before she began.

---

[4] Farad: a unit of capacitance (electricity-storing power) of a condenser.

ANNABELLE

A two-timing girl, Annabelle,
Was well known as a Jezebel.
But you lack in tact
If you write down that fact
And might be sued for libel.

ANNETTE

A society girl called Annette
Set up house in a smart maisonette.
But they thought her uncouth
When she climbed on the roof
Clad only in red flannelette.

ANNIE

There once was a Scots girl called Annie
Who, like her ilk, was quite canny,
She'd earn a bawbee
From a poor refugee
By doing a stint as a nanny.

ANNIS

A sporty young girl called Annis
Always sought her model Adonis.
She knew at a glance
When she found him by chance
Just playing a game of lawn tennis.

ANTHEA

A flighty young girl called Anthea
Would meet up with men here and there.
She'd greet them in places
Such as dancehalls and races,
Or often just any old where.

ANTHONY (ALSO ANTONY)

> A voracious young man called Anthony
> Was known for his considerable gluttony.
> When he changed his venue,
> He'd go through the menu
> Because it relieved the monotony.

ANTOINETTE

> There was a young actress – Antoinette,
> Who choked on a potato croquette.
> Unlike her namesake
> Who told them, "Eat cake!"
> She survived, and went back on set.

ANTONIA

> My fickle girlfriend called Antonia
> Went down with the dreaded pneumonia.
> While she convalesced
> She made a new conquest.
> Then said, "Don't call me; I'll phone yer."

ANTONY. SEE ANTHONY.

APRIL

> An ambitious singer called April
> Lived not too far from Cape Rill.
> She said, "Can you tell
> If I sang that song well?"
> I said, "No, but I'm sure the tape will."

ARCH

> An extremely young soldier called Arch
> Once climbed up a rather tall larch.
> He was put on a charge
> By his company sarge,
> And sent on a very long march.

ARCHIBALD

A redheaded man – Archibald,
Once said, "I know what I'm called.
It is really not fair
To refer to my hair,
And when you do, I'm appalled."

ARCHIE (ALSO ARCHY)

A would-be concert artist called Archie
Was told his performance was starchy.
"Your technique was scanty
And you played it *andante*
When it clearly says the tempo's *vivace*."

ARIADNE

There was a lame girl – Ariadne,
Who had a very bad knee.
She used as a prop
The stick from a mop.
Before that she only had *me*.

ARLENE

A silly young girl called Arlene
Said she'd like to be queen.
But she thought it a crime
There was no overtime
So now she's not nearly so keen.

ARNIE

There was a young tenor called Arnie
Who came from the town of Kilarnie.
He would sing a song
And often go wrong
But cover the fact with blarney.

ARTHUR

An experimental chemist called Arthur
Once obtained a measure of sulphur.
With a charcoal goo
Plus KNO_2,[5]
He lit a fuse. Now Arthur's just half a.

ASHLEY (ALSO ASHLEIGH)

A holidaymaker called Ashley
Wore some hot pants quite rashly.
The sun did burn
Her skin to a turn,
But she carried on unabashedly.

ATHALSTAN

There once was a Dane – Athalstan,
Who was never much of a man.
He would sit in a chair
Just combing his hair
And drink wine from an old tin can.

ATHALSTANE

There was another young man – Athalstane,
Who sartorially was rather vain.
So we told him that
He should not wear a hat,
Especially when driving a train.

ATHANASIOUS

There once was an Athanasious
Who always seemed ostentatious.
He never seemed grateful
And became quite hateful;
He really was most ungracious.

---

[5] KNO_2: gunpowder.

AUBERON

There was a young chemist – Auberon,
Who worked with some yellow boron.
He tried to anneal
The stuff with some steel
But found he'd done it all wrong.

AUBREY

Said an old store keeper called Aubrey,
"I sell Cheddar, Stilton or Brie.
My children, I feed 'em
On two types of Edam,
It's so good for them and for me."

AUDREY

There was a young girl called Audrey
Whose style of dress was quite tawdry.
And what is worse
She spoke in verse,
And her words were always so bawdry.[6]

AUGUSTIN

A dirty old man called Augustin
Had habits quite digustin'.
But his house was clean,
And quite pristine,
'Cos his wife was always a-dustin'.

AUGUSTUS

There was a young crook called Augustus
Who tried his very best to bust us.
We got very bored
With his attempts at fraud,
But it's his lies that always disgust us.

---

[6] Bawdry: (archaic) obscene language.

AURELIA

A genius of a girl called Aurelia
Once grew a giant lobelia.
In ten years it curled
Right round the world
And finished up here in Murelia.

AURELIAN

A roving young man called Aurelian
Applied to become an Australian.
But they turned him down
With a solemn frown
Because he was so saturnalian.

AURORA

A young Spanish girl called Aurora
Tried to study fauna and flora;
But instead of this
She discovered bliss
When she wed and became a Señora.

AUSTEN (ALSO AUSTIN)

There was a young athlete called Austen
Who always said that he must win.
He would set a fast pace
In every run race,
But always would tie with his twin.

AVA

There was a young girl called Ava
Who decided to become a caver.
She got lost underground,
Took two days to be found,
But they said that no one was braver.

AVRIL

A foolish young girl called Avril
Had an IQ in the region of nil.
She took the wrong train,
And arrived in Spain
Instead of at Kingston Dev'rill.

AYLWIN (ALSO AYLWYN)

There was a young man called Aylwin
Who disguised himself as his twin.
He fooled his own porpoise
And not his twin's tortoise
Which bit him quite hard in the shin.

B

There was a young novice called Bardolph…

BABETTE

An Australian girl called Babette
Was quite a creature of habit.
There was kangaroo
On the Monday menu,
And on Sundays it was always rabbit.

BABS

There was a young chemist called Babs
Who worked in one of those labs.
But she gave listeria
To her blue wisteria,
Because she'd forgotten its jabs.

BAILEY

A hard-working artiste called Bailey
Played Bach on his ukulele.
His Mass in B Minor
Went well in China
When played *giocoso*, i.e. gaily.

BALDIE

A lazy young Scot called Baldie
Started work one day in Kilcaldy.
But the boss said, "You're slow,
I think you must go,
'Cos yon task took you nearly all dee."

BALTHASAR (ALSO BALTHAZAR)

There was an Iranian called Balthasar
Who was told to go and bathe the Shah.
He took the plunge,
Picked up a sponge;
But instead, set to work on his car.

BARBIE

A cheese-loving girl called Barbie
Was arrested by the police near Derby.
The proceedings were short
When she was brought to court
And found guilty of stealing our Brie.

BARDOLPH

There was a young novice called Bardolph
Who went to a club to learn golf.
He thought he'd go nuts
When he missed all his putts,
And said worm casts put him right off.

BARNARD

There was a young man called Barnard
Who was really a bit of a card.
He went too far
With a rude circular
And found himself feathered and tarred.

BARNEY

There was a young vagrant called Barney
Whose talk was full of blarney.
He couldn't care less
For appearance or dress,
And his socks were all holey and darny.

BARRY

There was a young Scot called Barry
Who wore a purple Glengarry.
The extraordinary sight
Put the girls to flight,
So he never ever did marry.

BART

A rather odd man called Bart
Always looked terribly smart.
But the girls stayed clear
When he came near
For he travelled by horse-drawn cart.

BARTHOLOMEW

There was a young man – Bartholomew,
Whose dog made its flying debut:
It managed to enter
A space flight centre,
And they made it one of the crew.

BASIL

I once had a neighbour called Basil
Who was always going on the razzle.
And the tum tum tum
Of his wretched drum
Wore my nerves to a frazzle.

BAUBIE

There was a Scots girl called Baubie
Who was told her paintings were dauby.
She threw a half brick
At the myopic critic,
And took herself off to Corby.

BEA

There was a young girl called Bea
Who lived in a hut by the sea.
I don't dare to mention
The internal dimension
But that place could not include me.

BEATRICE

There was a young girl called Beatrice
Who took off her ring and said, "This
Is always a sign
Of male design,
But I've decided to stay a Miss."

BEAU

There was a young man called Beau
Who was really quite nice to know.
If your battery was flat
He'd give you a pat
And say, "Come on, I'll give you a tow."

BECK

There was a young duchess called Beck
Who looked a bit of a wreck.
She had streaks of mascara
All over her tiara,
And a wart on the side of her neck.

BECKY

A cross-eyed girl called Becky
Had eyes that were deep-set and flecky.
When asked what she saw,
She said, "It's a bore,
But things look all broken and specky."

BEE

There was a young girl called Bee
Who said to her friend named Dee,
"We're both abbreviations
Which saves some complications
So that's why I'm a B. See D?"

BELINDA

Said a motor-cycling girl called Belinda,
"My ignition is burnt to a cinder.
I knew by the pong
That something was wrong.
Should I have put oil in the cylinder?"

BELLA

Theer wuz a yung girl called Bella
Who used to be a very poor spella.
She worked in some banks
And rote letters of fanks,
Butt they never maid her a tella.

BEN

A high-flying professor called Ben,
Had knowledge quite beyond my ken.
He'd talk about photons
And atoms and protons…
I wish he'd come down to earth now and then.

BENEDICT

There was a young child – Benedict,
Who was told by her mum, "Don't contradict!
You're not all that bad,
And I know it's a fad
But I tell you it's off you are ticked."

BENEDICTA

There was a young woman called Benedicta
Who changed when a young crook picked her.
It's all too droll,
But she became his moll,
And remained so until somebody nicked her.

BENJAMIN

There was a stunt man called Benjamin,
Who said, "Please just call me Danger Min."
They said, "You mean, *man*?"
"Well, that was my plan,
But my tongue and my mind keep on jammin'."

BENNETT

An ambitious young man called Bennett
Claimed he wanted to enter the senate.
But they said, "Examine yourself,
It's people not pelf,
And you must remember that tenet."

BERENICE

A ghastly young girl called Berenice
Was known to most as my "terror-niece".
She'd pull the boys' hair
And make them all swear.
But her mum said 'twas just her caprice.

BERNADETTE

A lonesome young a girl – Bernadette,
Met up with a lonely vedette.
She said, "Let's go out."
He replied, "Not with my gout.
You'd far better find a cadet."

BERNIE

A gambling young man called Bernie
Won lots of money on Ernie.
He spent the lot
On a thirty-foot yacht,
But it sank on its first deep-sea journey.

BERT (ALSO BURT)

There was a quiet young man called Bert
Who some people thought was inert.
He'd never reply,
To the question "Why?"
In fact he was really most curt.

BERTRAM

There was a young man called Bertram
Who discovered a small hurt ram.
He persuaded a tup
To hold it up
While he sent off a quick telegram.

BERYL

An impulsive young girl called Beryl
Once put herself in great peril.
She stroked the hair
Of a grizzly bear.
Alas! Not a tame one, but feral.

BESS

There was a pretty girl called Bess.
And what she did was anyone's guess.
It might be true
That some men knew,
For she always answered "Yes".

BESSIE

There was a young blonde called Bessie
Whose hair was long and very tressy.
An enormous loop
Would fall in her soup
And the result was always so messy.

BETSY

There is an old girl called Betsy,
Whose age is, er, well now, let's see –
It is twice my own,
And I'm an old crone;
Let's just say she's not jetsy.

BETTINA

There was a young girl called Bettina
Who played an outsized concertina.
It gave us pain
As we saw her strain
And watched her get greener and greener.

BETTY

A pasta-loving girl called Betty
Had views on life that were petty.
When she got in a huff
She'd go and take snuff,
Then eat lots and lots of spaghetti.

BEVAN

There was a young batsman called Bevan
Who was in his school's first eleven.
They needed eight to win
And he was last man in –
But he managed to make only seven.

BEVERLEY

There was a bright spark called Beverley
Who solved problems so cleverly.
But it caused great strain
On her remarkable brain,
And taxed her resources too heavily.

BEVIS

There was a young man called Bevis
Who got lost when climbing Ben Nevis.
When the rescuers came,
He took the blame,
But they secretly thought him a menace.

BILL

There was a young author called Bill
Who always used pens with a quill.
A shortage of geese
From a fowl disease
Reduced all his output to nil.

BILLY

There was a young fop called Billy
Who looked extremely silly.
For his opera hat
Was squashed quite flat
As he walked down Piccadilly.

BINNIE

There was a young girl called Binnie
Who was proud of her brand new mini.
They said, "It's too fast."
Which made her aghast.
"Then I'll change my new skirt for a pinny."

BLODWEN

There was a young pullet called Blodwen
Who was strutting one day in the quad, when
Along came a lizard
Which bit her gizzard,
And we all saw plenty of blood then.

BO

There was a fast girl called Bo
Whose life was really all go!
When a man cried, "Flee,
To Gretna Green with me!"
She said, "I'll stick to the status quo."

BOB

There was a young man called Bob
Who could not obtain a job.
Then he won the pools,
Bought lots of jewels,
And became a terrible snob.

BORIS

There was a married student called Boris
Who decided to study Horace.
But he'd always use Latin
To call his cat in.
No wonder he was deserted by Doris.

BRADLEY

There is a young man called Bradley
Who seldom does anything badly.
While at Noughts and Crosses
He knows who the boss is
But at Bridge, he beats me – sadly!

BRAIN

There was never a man called Brain.
It's that wretched typist, Jane.
She transposed an 'I' with an 'A',
And whatever I say
She's bound to do it again.

BRANDY

There was a young man we called Brandy
Who was losing his hair, which was sandy.
There was a temptation
To make the observation
That he was starting to look quite like Ghandi.

BRENDA

A naïve young girl called Brenda
Used to send food to the prisoner of Zenda.
They said she was mad,
But she just said, "I'm glad,
Now he can go on a bender."

BRENDAN

There was a young runner called Brendan
Who pulled his Achilles tendon.
With a small piece of leather
He joined it together.
He's just the sort you depend on.

BRIAN (ALSO BRYAN)

There was a young man called Brian,
Who was really as brave as a lion.
When he met a tiger
On the face of the Eiger,
He threw it halfway to Zion.

BRIDGET

There was a young girl called Bridget
Who was always inclined to fidget.
The underlying cause
Was the microscopic jaws
Of an invisible but voracious widget.

BRIDIE

A fastidious young girl called Bridie
Was always so terribly tidy.
If a man moved a chair,
From here to there,
She'd ask if he were bona fide!

BRIONY

A tough-minded girl called Briony
Once said with considerable irony:
"I may look quite weak,
But I have a hard streak,
So don't vent your ire on me."

BRITT

There was an old lady called Britt
Who showed remarkable grit.
When attacked by a dove
She gave it a shove
And sent its owner a writ.

BRODERICK

A hay-making farmer called Broderick,
Said, "Now at last I've godda rick;
So, as well as my seed
I have all my feed,
And I can select which fodder I pick."

BRONWEN

An aspiring young actress called Bronwen
Had a few drinks with some con-men.
When they told her some fables,
She turned the tables,
And made off with what they had on them.

BRUCE

There was a young student called Bruce
Who seemed to be somewhat obtuse.
To make him astuter
I lent him a computer
But he said it wasn't much use.

BRUNO

There was a young man called Bruno
Who liked to listen to Gounod.
When he got bored,
With an old record,
He'd dream about Faust – and you know…

BRYAN. SEE BRIAN.

BUCK

A feather in his hat had Buck,
Who was always out of his luck.
When out for a walk
He was attacked by a hawk
'Cos he looked like a mallard duck.

BUD

A young private soldier called Bud
Was always lying around in the mud.
He once threw a grenade
At an enemy brigade,
But it turned out to be just a dud.

BUDDY

There was a young soldier called Buddy
Who, like his friend, got muddy.
He'd wash his cheek
In the nearest creek,
He was really so fuddy-duddy.

BUNTY

There was a young pig called Bunty
Who was full of life but grunty.
She ate her swill
With a hearty will,
But not too much, she was runty.

BURT. SEE BERT.

BUSTER

A young astronaut called Buster
Had trouble with his retro-thruster.
He was within an ace
Of heading through space
To an ancient and distant star cluster.

BUTCH

An old Yorkshire man was Butch.
He came from the north, and as such
His vowels would reflect
His own dialect.
His syntax was good, but not much.

BYRON

There was a young alto called Byron
Who liked the sound of a siren.
He tried to sing
In tune with that thing,
But it sounded like 'Any Old Iron'!

C

There was an old witch called Caitlin...

CAELIA (ALSO CELIA)

A new-fangled medic called Caelia
Was trained never ever to feel yer.
She cured by radiation
And some prestidigitation,
But was always able to heal yer.

CAESAR

There was an old soldier called Caesar
Who declared he would conquer Pisa.
He assembled some legions
From all of the regions,
But forgot to apply for a visa.

CAITLIN

There was an old witch called Caitlin
Who wrote the epitaph for her late kin:
I COULD NOT SEE
THE REACTION THERE'D BE
IF YOU MIX GUNPOWDER IN A CAKE TIN.

CALLUM

A short-sighted chemist called Callum
Once swallowed a packet of alum.
He developed a cough
And his ears dropped off
While his nose went the colour of plum.

CAMERON

An aspiring orator called Cameron
Tried hard, but tended to stammer on.
They first tried a tutor
As a sort of trouble-shooter,
But just had to bring a crammer on.

CAMILLA

A rather immature girl called Camilla
Took a lease on a lovely French villa.
She was not really pro
The new-fangled euro,
And didn't understand the cedilla.

CANDIA

There was a young child called Candia
Who claimed her playpen was handier;
"So please Mummy, please,
May I invite Tom and Louise?"
And her mother said, "Why, yes, you can dear."

CANDIDA

A damsel in distress called Candida
Was tied up by a thug who hid her.
Along came a knight
Who, espying her plight,
Took out his sword and undid her.

CAREY

There is an ugly man called Carey
About whom opinions vary.
At work he's known
To set the right tone
In contrast, his friends think he's scary.

CARL (ALSO KARL)

A rough-voiced man called Carl
Spoke all his words with a snarl.
The sound began to vex us,
So we offered him to Texas.
But they said he was much too banal.

CARLA

There was a young fly called Carla
Who buzzed off to the local gala.
We've all heard who she met
With his silken sticky net,
And enticed her into his parlour.

CARLOTTA

A naïve young girl called Carlotta
Fell for an awful old rotter.
He flew her to Spain
In his private aeroplane,
Met someone else and forgot her.

CARMEL

An apprentice cook called Carmel
Was told to shake the jar well.
But she let out a scream
When the salad cream
Shot out and enclosed her in gel.

CARMEN

There was a town girl called Carmen
Who decided to take up farmin'.
They said, "Now milk a cow!"
She said, "Okay, but how?
I find the prospect alarmin'."

CAROL (ALSO CAROLE)

There was a young walker called Carol,
Who said she'd just seen a troll.
She suffered disillusion
From the optical illusion,
For it turned out to be just a knoll.

CAROLYN

A look-alike girl – Carolyn,
Was, like her four sisters, a quin.
She had to strive
To count up to five
But didn't know where to begin.

CARRIE

A very bad cook called Carrie
Most earnestly wanted to marry.
But she wanted a guy
Who could bake her a pie,
And not any Tom, Dick or Harry.

CARYS

A short-sighted girl called Carys
Was invited to Buckingham Palace.
On arriving there
She tripped on a stair
And crashed into a statue of Paris.[7]

CASS

There was a young milkmaid called Cass
Who owned an intelligent ass.
It knew its times table
But was never quite able
To understand the meaning of mass.

CASSIE

There was a film extra called Cassie
Who had a canine-like chassis.
She could run on all fours
And had rather large jaws,
So was used as a stand-in for Lassie.

---

[7] Paris: a Trojan prince, son of Priam.

CATHARINE (ALSO CATHERINE, KATHARINE, KATHERINE, AND KATHRYN)

A ravenous young girl – Catharine –
Dined only on atherine;[8]
This is sold as smelt
In the northern veldt,
But she restricted her meal to the skin.

CATHIE (ALSO CATHY, KATHI, KATHIE, AND KATHY)

There was a young lady called Cathie,
Whose figure was ever so lathy.
When I said what I thought
She got quite overwrought.
Now I know she can also be wrathy.

CATRIONA

A Hebridian girl called Catriona
Died when the wind blew a tree on 'er.
By public subscription
There was a lovely inscription
On the statue they raised in Iona.

CECIL

There was a young chemist called Cecil
Who was left in charge of a vessel.
But the ship went aground,
So he was once again found
Back with his mortar and pestle.

---

[8] Atherine: a type of fish.

CECILIA

A blue-stockinged girl called Cecilia
Had read all the works of Elia.
And she found an anagram
For this man, Charles Lamb,
But she thought it was too familiar.

CEDRIC

A man of statistics called Cedric
Once said, "I am quite polyhedric.
There are sides to me
That are hard to see,
The rest is quite academic."

CELESTE

An athletic young girl called Celeste
Was ever so full of zest.
She was so inspiring
We found it quite tiring
And wished she'd give things a rest.

CELESTINE

There was a young girl – Celestine,
Who started to slowly turn green.
She realised her peril,
When she became deep beryl
And claimed it was caused by a gene.

CELIA. SEE CAELIA.

CHARITY

An aspiring young actress called Charity
Was noted for her jocularity.
But she couldn't win
For she was tall and thin
And an example of angularity.

Charles

There was an old farmer called Charles
Who kept pigs and sheep and fowls.
There was some dispute
As to who owned the fruit,
And everyone said it was Carl's.

Charlotte

A supple young girl called Charlotte
Once tied herself into a knot.
Some said the reef
Was beyond belief,
Others that she deserved what she got.

Charmaine (also Sharmaine)

There was a young girl called Charmaine
Who we thought was somewhat arcane.
And if I'm not wrong
Her name lives in song,
Which has made her terribly vain.

Chas

There was a young chemist called Chas
Who fell in a sticky morass.
He said as the ooze
Rose up to his shoes,
"What an interesting biomass!"

Chastity

A brash young girl called Chastity
Showed far too much audacity.
She once told a bishop
That he smelt of hyssop
And accused him of too much laxity.

CHELSEA

There was a young nurse called Chelsea
Who worked for a firm (plc),
If you got ill
They'd get you a pill
And a sister to give TLC.[9]

CHERIE (ALSO CHERRY)

There was a girl soldier called Cherie
Who was detailed to be an equerry.
She looked very staid
All decked in braid,
But was demoted for trying to make merry.

CHESTER

A jolly young man called Chester
Had a cap made of green polyester.
It was just as well
That he owned a bell,
For they made him the new court jester.

CHLOE

A back-packing girl called Chloe
Was in NZ with her friend named Zoë.
A Maori said, "We'll pay you
To climb up Ruapehu,
But don't ever try Ngaurhoe."[10]

---

[9] TLC: Tender Loving Care.

[10] Ruapehu and Ngaurhoe: two mountains in New Zealand.

CHRIS

There was a young person called Chris
Who said, "The world is like this:
It's a sphere made of soil
And silicon and oil
And lots of things I won't miss."

CHRISSIE (ALSO CHRISSY)

A pretty young girl called Chrissie
Was alleged to be a little bit prissy.
But I know for a fact
It was just an act
And in truth she was really quite kissy!

CHRISTIAN

There was a young rider called Christian
Who was known as a bold equestrian.
But a fall at a jump
Gave him a bump,
So now he's just a pedestrian.

CHRISTIE (ALSO CHRISTY)

There was a young curate called Christie
Who worked in the church sacristy.
"A rhyme for my name,"
He said, "Would bring fame
But I've got it at last – it's *misty*!"

CHRISTINA

There was a plump girl called Christina
Who decided to become a gleaner.
She got quite profane
When picking up grain
But the exercise made her much leaner.

CHRISTOBEL

A learned young girl called Christobel
Thought that life was a mere bagatelle.
With some taciturnity
She said that eternity
Had a secret that she just wouldn't tell.

CHRISTOPHER

There was a young scholar called Christopher
Who wanted to become a philosopher.
But he became no fan
Of the thoughts of man,
So decided to become a gastrosopher.[11]

CHRISTY. SEE CHRISTIE.

CHRYSTAL

There was a girl soldier called Chrystal
Who was an expert shot with a pistol.
But she was put on a charge
By her apoplectic sarge
When she consistently tried to miss drill.

CICILY

An energetic old lady called Cicily
Would always behave so busily.
She could dance a gavotte
Eating apple charlotte
While twirling around quite dizzily.

---

[11] Gastrosopher: one skilled in the art of good eating.

CILLA

There once was a schoolgirl called Cilla
Who would never use the cedilla.
She drove me quite mad
'Cos her French was so bad
I really thought I would kill her!

CINDY (ALSO SINDY)

There was a young tourist called Cindy
Who went off to Rawalpindi.
But she left quite soon
In a bad monsoon,
Because it was much too windy.

CIS (ALSO SIS)

A dotty young girl called Cis
Used to worship the god known as Dis.[12]
Now, he can be found
In the across and down
Of puzzles – and rhymes like this.

CISSIE (ALSO CISSY, SISSIE AND SISSY)

There was an old lady called Cissie
Who used to drive a tin lizzie.
In a kind of daze
She set out for Hayes
But arrived in Mevagissy.

CLAIR (ALSO CLAIRE AND CLARE)

A high-wire girl we called Clare
Always worked for a travelling fair.
She used a trapeze
With the greatest of ease
Whilst eating a chocolate éclair.

---

[12] Dis: a name for Pluto; hence the infernal world.

CLANCY

There was a young seaman called Clancy
Who paddled a canoe up the Yangtze.
When he reached Nanking,
He said, "It's a curious thing
But it's not the type of place I fancy."

CLARA

There was an old hag called Clara
And they said there was no one queerer;
She lived in a ditch
With a one-eyed witch
And screamed if you came too near her.

CLARE. SEE CLAIR.

CLARENCE

A young accountant called Clarence
Was a man of very few talents.
He received no plaudits
When he did audits
For he never made any books balance.

CLARICE

A generous young girl called Clarice
Used to live in the middle of Paris.
If you lost a coin
In the Bois de Boulogne
She'd give you another one gratis.

CLARINDA

There once was a car named Clarinda
Which fired on only one cylinder.
How the owner fussed
Over this heap of rust!
In the end it was burnt to a cinder.

CLARISSA

A young schoolgirl called Clarissa
Was so small you could almost miss her.
She was top of her class
But oh dear and alas!
She could never understand the mantissa.

CLARK (ALSO CLARKE)

A genius of a man called Clark
Used to specialise in the quark.
But an electric charge
Got much too large,
Which finished this bright young spark.

CLAUD (ALSO CLAUDE)

A member of the staff called Claud
Was all his firm could afford.
But for his devotion,
They gave him promotion,
And an unpaid seat on the board.

CLAUDETTE

A fast young deb called Claudette
Got much too deeply in debt.
She slammed her door
In the face of the law
And escaped to Brazil by jet.

CLAUDIUS

There was a dull man called Claudius
Who, they said, always bored us.
His wife Messalina
Was very much meaner,
And it was she who overawed us.

CLEM

There was a young jeweller called Clem
Who acquired a beautiful gem.
When he cut the faces
They formed the bases
Of a glittering diadem.

CLEMENT

There was a young student called Clement
Who thought he'd found a new element.
He made a claim,
But took the blame
When it turned out just to be sediment.

CLEMENTINE

There was an old girl – Clementine,
Who claimed she was just twenty-nine.
But I took one look
And said, "Not in my book,
She'll never be my Valentine."

CLEO

There was a young soldier called Cleo
Who was brought up before her CO.
She was reduced in rank
For driving a tank
Into the village and through the PO.

CLIFF

There was an old man called Cliff
Who wore his hair in a quiff.
He dyed it brown
To hide his frown,
And to smother his awful sniff.

CLIO

A busking young girl called Clio
Went and hitch-hiked her way to Rio.
She strummed on a banana
In the Copacabana,
And then formed a musical trio.

CLIVE

A young entrepreneur called Clive
Was known for his determined drive.
He'd buy out firms
On bargain terms,
And manage to make them all thrive.

CLODAGH

An athletic young girl called Clodagh
Climbed up a Chinese pagoda.
Then stood on one hand
While conducting a band
And drinking a whisky soda.

CLOTHILDA (ALSO CLOTILDA)

A young housewife called Clothilda
Employed a new cowboy builder.
He built a wall
Just ten feet tall
But it collapsed and nearly killed her.

COLEEN

There was a young girl called Coleen
Who was a friend of an African Queen.
She travelled in style
Down the length of the Nile
In an amphibious limousine.

COLETTE (ALSO COLLETTE)

An exotic young dancer – Colette,
Was given a new castanet.
She said, "It's hypnotic
But much too exotic
I might like it in time – but not yet."

COLIN

There was a young athlete called Colin
Who said, "I've run ten miles, I'm all in.
And I think I'm gaining
From all this training,
But it's worth it if I can win."

COLUMBUS

There was a young sailor named Columbus,
Who created quite an old rumpus.
He had an aberration
With astro-navigation,
And built a small 3-D rhombus.

CONNOR

There was a young child called Connor
Whose very first words were, "I wanna…"
At a ripe old age
He turned the last page,
And his final words were, "I'm a gonner."

CONRAD (ALSO CONRADE AND KONRAD)

Said a small boy called Conrad,
"I didn't know where you'd gone Dad."
"I went to the shop
To buy you a chop;
That fish I bought you's gone bad."

CONSTANCE

There was a young schoolgirl called Constance
Who tended to confuse her consonants.
Her vowels she knew
From A to U,
But her essays were nothing but nonsense.

CORA

There was a young lady called Cora.
I would like to say I adore her,
But when I was bold
She was quite cold,
So all I do now is ignore her.

CORDELIA

There was a fat girl called Cordelia
Who ate buns and just got greedier.
When she finally burst
It was reported first
To her friends, then on the media.

CORIN

There was a blind beggar called Corin
Who was given a brand new florin.
He flung it down
And said with a frown,
"That ain't no good, it looks foreign."

CORNELIUS

There was a young quack called Cornelius
Who said he was sure he could heal us.
He gave us a cure
Which didn't look pure,
And made us feel almost bilious.

COSMO

There was a young chef called Cosmo
Who asked me how to make moss grow.
I said, "You're a clot,
A gardener you're not,
So go on kneading your dough!"

CRAIG

There was a young Scot called Craig
Who spent one night near Malaig.
When I asked him where,
He said, "I don't really care."
But then he was always so vague.

CRESSIDA

There was a young girl – Cressida,
Who met the Egyptian sidar.
He said, "You know the Sphinx?
Well, on Sundays it winks."
But he found it quite easy to kid her.

CRISPIN

A peculiar young man called Crispin
Always put jam on his Disprin.
And furthermore
He'd buy a whole score,
Then give them all a good whiskin'.

CRYSTAL

There was a French girl called Crystal
Who kept under her dress… a pistol!
In la Rue Canebière,
This gave us a scare
When her skirt was blown up by the Mistral.

CUTHBERT

There was a fellow called Cuthbert
Whom they said was an old stuffed shirt.
He shortened his name
But he was still the same –
He was even more pompous and curt.

CYNTHIA

There was a old soak called Cynthia
Who'd sit in a pub and drink gin there.
If they turned her out
She would start to shout
And neighbours would call, "Less din there!"

CYRIL

There once was a creature called Cyril
Who put his own life in some peril.
When he wanted to flee,
He would climb up a tree,
"After all," he would say, "I'm a squirrel."

D

There was a mechanic called Diana…

DAI

A nosy young man called Dai
Was always asking me, "Why?"
Then he'd go and natter
About another matter
So he would never hear my reply.

DAISY

A confused young girl called Daisy
Once said, "I'm a little bit hazy.
Did we go to Dallas
Or to Blenheim Palace?
Or perhaps it was both, and I'm crazy."

DAMIEN

There was a old man called Damien
Who behaved like a bold Bohémian.
Please note the acute
And pronounce to suit.
Yes it's wrong and certainly alien.

DAMON

A famous old man called Damon
Had a plaque on a wall with his name on.
He saved his town,
When the dam fell down,
And that's what he built his fame on.

DAN

There was a young Aussie called Dan
Who drank tea from an old billy-can.
On the banks of the Murray,
He would eat his curry,
Which he mixed with a chocolate flan.

DANA (PRONOUNCED DAHN-AH)

There was a young rambler called Dana,
Who walked all the way to Ghana.
But the cocoa she drank
She said was quite rank.
So they gave her a chocolate sultana.

DANDY

There was a young jockey called Dandy
Whose legs were short and so bandy.
And naturally, of course,
They encircled his horse
In a manner that was really quite handy.

DANIEL

There was a young child called Daniel
Who was given a Christmas annual.
He gained the knowledge,
That saw him through college,
And produced his own auto manual.

DANIELLE

A young football fan called Danielle
Said, "My friends and I – can we yell!
When our striker scored
How we all roared!
But groaned in despair when he fell."

DANNY

> There was a young tipster called Danny
> Who made thousands for his old granny.
> He went to the races,
> And foretold all the places.
> His clairvoyance was really uncanny.

DAPHNE

> There was a young cook called Daphne
> Who worked at the local NAAFI,
> She said, "I'd call it quits
> If I could work at the Ritz;
> I must find out if they'd have me."

DARIUS

> The King of Persia called Darius[13]
> Found that life was much too precarious.
> He could conquer Thrace,
> But was put in his place,
> For Marathon was much more serious.

DARLEEN (ALSO DARLENE)

> A brash young girl called Darleen
> Had just survived Halloween.
> "I went out," she said,
> "To paint the town red.
> But some people made such a scene!"

DARYL (ALSO DARRYL)

> There was an old actor called Daryl
> Who took part in *A Christmas Carol*.
> The part of Scrooge,
> He said, was huge,
> As he doled out cash from a barrel.

---

[13] Darius was defeated at the Battle of Marathon by the Greeks.

DAVE

A reckless young man called Dave
Was quite unable to save.
He made quite a hash
Of investing his cash,
And was forced to live in a cave.

DAVID

There was a young sportsman called David
Whose views on golf were quite avid.
The tales of his swings,
Bored princes and kings,
And about slices he got really rabid.

DAWN

There was an old lady called Dawn
Who went out to mow her lawn.
"But where is the cutter?"
She was heard to mutter.
"Don't tell me the darned thing has gawn."

DEAN (ALSO DEANE)

A bewildered young man called Dean
Once said, "I'll have to come clean.
I'll be quite explicit
And say that I did it,
But I'm not quite sure what I mean."

DEANNA

A girl on safari called Deanna
Got lost out in the savannah.
She found a tree
Where food was free,
For it exuded a form of manna.

DEB

A happy young girl called Deb
Was born at the end of Feb.
So she was a Pisces
And quite used to crises,
And never felt at a low ebb.

DEBBIE (ALSO DEBBY)

A rather simple girl called Debbie
Was thought to be rather plebby.
She'd stand near the sea
Not far from me
And say, "Look at the tide, it's all ebby!"

DEBORAH

A society girl called Deborah
Had friends who did implore her:
"Don't marry yet
You've only just met.
You don't want to lose that deb aura."

DEE

A university girl called Dee
Was introduced three times to me.
Each time she forgot
My name – what a clot!
And to think she took a degree!

DELIA

A rather sick girl called Delia
Suffered from haemophilia.
I told her, "Take care
When cutting your hair
It's not so easy to heal yer."

DELILAH

There was a young girl called Delilah
Who said everyone tried to revile her.
She was quite a lass,
If a little bit crass,
So I did my best to beguile her.

DEMELZA

There is an old girl called Demelza
Who does what everyone tells her.
She's meek and mild
Like a very young child
And when she's bad her nurse quells her.

DEMI

A rather plump woman called Demi
Went to live in a very small semi.
To get in at all
She makes herself small,
And uses her pocket-sized jemmy.

DENIS (ALSO DENNIS)

A fractious young man called Denis
Once went on a bus ride to Venice.
He thought it banal,
So dammed a canal.
He really was quite a menace!

DENISE

A girl with a cold called Denise
Once gave an enormous sneeze.
The long protraction
Of the jet reaction
Took her up and into the trees.

DENNI

There was a poor girl called Denni
Who hoarded every last penny.
She put them in socks,
Which she kept in a box;
But I'm afraid there weren't very many.

DENNIS. SEE DENIS.

DENNY

A bright young man called Denny
Had qualities that were many.
He could fly a plane,
Or drive a train,
But was unable to woo young Jenny!

DEREK (ALSO DERRICK)

A peculiar man called Derek
Used to do things quite esoteric.
His most peculiar trait
Was to open a gate.
Then slam it in front of a cleric.

DERRY

A refined young man called Derry
Had a job as a royal equerry.
He would luxuriate
With heads of state
And drink their very best sherry.

DÉSIREE

I thought I knew about Désiree[14]
With the skin pink and smooth and airy.
But it's really quite true,
It was bad all through
And I was peeling this spud for my Mary.

DESMOND

An inane young man called Desmond
Said, "I'm in the Slough of Despond.
I'll wait for a drought
To get myself out."
So I quietly emptied his pond.

DETTA

A lovely old lady called Detta
Had a large and boisterous red setter.
She would stand on my toes
And lick my nose –
The dog I mean – when I let her.

DI

A flirtatious young lady called Di
Used to wink at me and say, "Hi!"
I asked her to sup
But she never turned up,
And now I ask myself, "Why?"

DIANA

There was a mechanic called Diana
Who was unable to move her spanner.
I helped her out
Like a real boy scout
By using her hat to fan her.

---

[14] Désiree: a type of potato.

DIANE (ALSO DIANNE)

> There was an old lady – Diane
> Who, I'm afraid to say, was my gran.
> She would spur me on
> Saying, "Well done, John!"
> Then tell me to get a brain scan.

DICK

> There was a young lad called Dick
> Whose neck developed a crick.
> They tried all night
> To put it right.
> Then knocked it straight with a brick.

DILYS

> A mathematical tyro called Dilys
> Said, "I think I know what nil is;
> I know it ought
> To be like nought,
> And as far as I know it still is."

DINA (ALSO DINAH)

> An American girl called Dina
> Was said to be from North Carolina.
> But in the song
> They got it wrong,
> She was really from Asia Minor.

DIONNE

> A time-travelling girl called Dionne
> Went off for a weekend in Bonn.
> She had time to spare
> For she wasn't there,
> Having arrived just after she'd gone.

DIRK

A fit young man called Dirk
Had only one outstanding quirk.
He could impress the men
(You can say that again!)
But he refused to take up work.

DODDY

There was a young lifeguard called Doddy
Who had a most beautiful body.
When the girls said, "Wow!"
Then ask him, "How?"
He'd say it was due to hot toddy.

DOL (ALSO DOLL)

A shipwrecked young dancer called Dol,
Was marooned on a coral atoll.
When she found half a mile
Was the extent of her isle
She'd sit on a rock 'n' roll.

DOLORES

There was a young student – Dolores
Who once met a very old war ace.
Her opinion of the hero
Was absolute zero
When she found he was seducing señores.

DOLLY

A female explorer called Dolly
Met a Chinaman who always said, "Solly."
"They're Rs not Ls!" she cried,
But the man just replied,
"So solly, now I'm off in my lolly."

DOMINIC (ALSO DOMINICK)

I had a young friend called Dominic
Who received a telegram: "BOMB IN NICK."
It was all go
Till they checked the PO,
The wire should have read: "TOM IN NICK."

DON

There was a young man we called Don
Whose pa was a lord, so was "Hon."
He lived in fear
Of becoming a peer,
For he felt he'd be ripe for a con.

DONALD

There was a vain man called Donald
Who found his head had gone bald.
He went to a quack
Who smeared on dried yak.
(The rest of the tale can't be told.)

DONNA

A suspicious young girl called Donna
Thought that I was trying to con her.
She said I'd taken
Her bit of bacon,
Despite giving my word of honour.

DONOVAN

A famous athlete called Donovan
Trained with his twin brother, Jonathan.
Perhaps that's the reason
In their very first season
They were equal first in the marathon

DORA

I knew a young girl called Dora
And I told her I was really all for her.
But she was quite curt
And I was so hurt.
That all I do now is ignore her.

DORCAS

There was an old woman called Dorcas
Whose voice was harsh and so raucous.
To avoid that sound,
We'd hide underground,
But she always managed to baulk us.

DOREEN

There was a young girl called Doreen
Who took a very large sniff of chlorine.
When we asked her why,
She started to cry,
Saying, "I thought it was a way to keep clean."

DORIS

An indolent young girl called Doris
Always enjoyed the scent of an orris.[15]
She would take a spray
And sniff it all day
While she sat in a chair called a Morris.[16]

---

[15] Orris: a type of iris.

[16] Morris: a type of chair with an adjustable reclining back.

DOROTHY

> An old-fashioned girl called Dorothy
> Once dreamt she'd met a horror flea.
> She said, "Don't bite!"
> To the little parasite,
> "Unless you want me to collar thee."

DOT

> The diminutive of Dorothy is Dot
> Which stops me looking a clot.
> You might think it mutilation
> To change the appellation,
> But it's easier to rhyme, that's what!

DOTTY

> There once was a girl called Dotty
> Who took a train to Lanzerote.
> When it reached the sea,
> She said, "Oh silly me!
> No wonder my friends think I'm potty."

DOUG (ALSO DUG)

> A funny little man called Doug
> Drank his wine from an old tin jug.
> But the chemical reaction
> Caused some putrefaction
> So he poured the rest on a slug.

DOUGLAS

> There was an old gardener called Douglas
> Who was told he ought to have dug less.
> He had killed the seeds
> Instead of the weeds;
> And, because of his age, he should tug less.

DREW

A pert young man called Drew
Bought his latest car brand-new.
When out on the loose
He just missed a goose;
So he stopped the car and said, "Boo!"

DRUCILLA (ALSO DRUSCILLA AND DRUSILLA)

There was a young girl – Drucilla,
Who was trained as a whisky distiller.
When she mixed a drachm[17]
With some strawberry jam,
They sent her right back to her villa.

DUDLEY

There was a rich man called Dudley
Who lived in a lane all puddly.
But he made quite a splash
With most of his cash,
And the girls thought him ever so cuddly.

DUG. SEE DOUG.

DULCIE

There was a young girl called Dulcie
Whose hair was said to be mousy.
But if you told her so
She'd get up and go.
And retort that you were just lousy.

---

[17] Drachm: a weight or measure formerly used by apothecaries.

DUNCAN

There was an old man called Duncan
Who said, "Two can do better than one can.
But with consistence
And some persistence,
Old ones do better than the young can."

DUSTIN

An apprentice metal worker called Dustin
Sought out some advice on rustin'.
They said, "Rub on enough
Of this very stuff,
But watch out, the smell is disgustin'!"

DWAINE

There was modern pirate called Dwaine
Who was ever so slightly insane.
While ashore in Tortuga
He pulled out his Luger,
And shot himself twice in the brain.

DWIGHT

There was an old soldier called Dwight
Who always did everything right.
His knowledge and tact
Were known for a fact,
And he lived in a house painted white.

DYLAN

There was an old crook called Dylan
Who stole a few tons of billon.[18]
But the fakes from his mint
Were all the wrong tint.
He was really a stupid old villain!

---

[18] Billon: an alloy used for making coins, medals and tokens.

DYLLIS

There was a young climber called Dyllis
Who said, "I wonder how high this hill is?"
It's getting darker,
And I see no marker,
Now where on earth are those gillies?"

E

A tardy young boy called Eddie...

EAMON

A religious man called Eamon
Once said, "I know I'm a layman,
But I'll sell my Rolls
And go to save souls
On the sun-soaked isle of Grand Cayman."

EARL (ALSO EARLE)

There is a young swain called Earl
Who is seeking the right sort of girl.
Her eyes must be blue
And the right sort of hue
And she must have a pretty kiss curl.

EARTHA

A business-like lady called Eartha
Claimed that she had bought Big Bertha.[19]
She sold it for scrap
To a keen young chap
To prop up a mine in old Merthyr.

EBEN

A precocious young child called Eben,
Said, "Ma, I can count up to seben."
Said Mum, "It's clear to see
That you take after me
For geniuses are made in heaben."

EBENEZER

A tough old Tuscan – Ebenezer,
Was known as a very loud sneezer.
His audible expirations
Were like detonations,
And that's why the tower leans at Pisa.

---

[19] Big Bertha: name for a German long-distance gun in WWI.

ECKY

A fastidious young man called Ecky
Divorced his wife called Becky.
Her omelets were tasty
As was her pastry,
But her pans were all crummy and specky.

ED

A pallid young man called Ed
Went off for a cruise in the Med.
On the second day out
He was struck down with gout
And never got out of his bed.

EDDIE (ALSO EDDY)

A tardy young boy called Eddie
Would never part with his teddy.
Whenever he was late
He would prevaricate,
And say that his bear wasn't ready.

EDGAR

An energetic young boy called Edgar
Used to play with his little old red car.
He wore himself out
And was heard to shout,
"Now I am going off to my bed, Ma!"

EDITH

A bed-ridden old lady called Edith
Found she had nothing to feed with.
But she found a string
Attached to a thing,
So she pulled it to see where it leadeth.

EDMUND

A humorous old man called Edmund
Was known as a man who had punned.
The "tail" of his life
Was spent in strife,
But of puns he had quite a fund.

EDNA

A pale young girl called Edna
Put on some rouge to redden 'er.
She used just enough
On her powder puff –
She had quite a wise old 'ed in 'er.

EDWARD

A meek young man called Edward
Felt he was nothing but deadwood.
But on reaching nineteen,
He became so keen
He scarcely had time to go bed-ward.

EDWIN

There was a young trader called Edwin
Who they said was forever peddlin'.
But he'd always interfere
Almost any old where
So you could say he was also meddlin'.

EDWINA

A fanatical old girl called Edwina
Thought she was a re-born Athena.
She would wave to Mars
And some of the stars
And hope that someone had seen her.

EGBERT

There was a lame sailor called Egbert
Who said that his new wooden leg hurt.
The sawbones unscrewed it
And then he renewed it
Saying that the trouble was peg-dirt.

EILEEN

There was a young girl called Eileen –
Well, younger than I am, I mean!
It might be naughty
To say she was forty,
But I'm sixty, so I'd better come clean!

EIRENE. SEE IRENE.

ELAINE

A slender young girl called Elaine
Was out one day in the rain,
But she slipped in the gutter
And was heard to mutter
Before disappearing right down the drain.

ELDRED

A colour-blind grocer – Eldred
Did his very best to sell bread.
To him flour was blue
And yeast was too,
While all of his buns were bright red.

ELEANOR (ALSO ELEANORE AND ELINOR)

An animal lover – Eleanor
Was not the one to ignore.
She kept a tame grampus[20]
In a tank by the campus,
Which annoyed everyone with its snore.

ELFREDA

A gardening girl called Elfreda
Was known as a very fast seeder.
It was not very gallant
To disparage her talent,
But they preferred a very fast weeder.

ELGIVA

There was a young babe called Elgiva
Who worked like a proverbial beaver.
That is to say,
She would spend all day
Just chewing away at her teether.

ELIAS

I had a young pupil called Elias
Who could not contain his bias.
He said, "You teachers
Are very odd creatures.
Who go out of their way to belie us."

---

[20] Grampus: a dolphin with a blunt snout and long pointed black flippers.

ELIJAH

A man who made soap was Elijah
And he kept his wares in a lye jar.[21]
But he got in a lather
When told by his father
That his goods were too pricey by far

ELINOR. SEE ELEANOR.

ELISABETH (ALSO ELIZABETH, LISBETH, AND LIZBETH)

In Canada, a young Elisabeth
Listened hard when the parson saith,
"Please don't go in there,
I can see a large bear!"
So she avoided a grisly death.

ELIZA

A thoughtless young girl called Eliza
Said that she admired the Kaiser.
But she was short of tact
When expressing that fact
So people were apt to despise her.

ELIZABETH. SEE ELISABETH.

ELLA

A brilliant young pianist called Ella
Used to play a bright tocatella.
For her skill with the pedal
They gave her a medal,
Which she wore on her left patella.

---

[21] Lye: a liquid used for washing. Hence lye soap.

ELLEN

There was a horticulturist called Ellen
Who had a garden centre in Welwyn.
She bred a new flower
In her secret bower.
But where it is, I'm not tellin'.

ELLIE

An eccentric young girl called Ellie
Always wore one clog and a wellie.
As she limped along
She would sing a rude song,
Or recite the poems of Shelley.

ELMER

Said a new young feller called Elmer,
"I've cut down this tree – it's an elm. Er…
I think that is so,
But I really don't know,
If I'm wrong I know I'll get hell, Ma."

ELOISA

A peculiar young girl, Eloisa,
Fell in love with a dirty old greaser.
She set him aflame
With her own pet name
And she always said, "Hullo Caesar!"

ELSA

There was a young maiden called Elsa,
Who said, "Why do you have to yell, sir?
At your own request,
I'm doing my best,
But I really have nothing to sell, sir!"

ELSIE

An army tearaway girl called Elsie
Didn't relish her posting to Chelsea.
She complained to the major
Who said, "You're a teenager;
You'll go!" But she snapped, "We'll see."

ELSPETH

A biblical girl we call Elspeth
Gambled with life and with death.
As an Ephraimite
She sealed her plight
By being unable to say shibboleth.

EMERY (ALSO EMORY)

A would-be musician called Emery
Always sticks in my memory.
He was known to strum
On an old kettle drum
In the Garden of Gethsemane.

EMILE

An ingenious young man called Emile
Invented a new type of wheel.
Although it was square,
It could bend here and there
And best of all it would self-seal.

EMILIA

A rather dotty girl called Emilia
Who went off to study anthelia.[22]
But when she got burnt
By suns that just weren't,
She changed to study aphelia.[23]

EMILY

An outrageous young girl called Emily
Always used scent that was lemony.
If one made a remark
She behaved like a tart
Saying, "It ain't as if it's a felony."

EMLYN

There was a young tourist called Emlyn
Who decided to visit the Kremlin.
When he arrived in Red Square
He was met by a bear
Disguised as a small Russian gremlin.

EMMA

There was a young girl called Emma
Who studied insects and their stemma.[24]
When she found that gnats
Wore gaiters and spats,
It gave her quite a dilemma.

---

[22] Anthelia: plural of anthelion. A luminous white halo-like area occasionally seen in the sky opposite the sun.

[23] Aphelia: plural of aphelion, the point on the orbit of a planet or comet that is farthest from the sun.

[24] Stemma: in this case, the simple eye of an insect.

EMMANUEL (ALSO IMMANUEL)

There is a young author – Emmanuel,
Who writes tales for a children's annual.
His subject is dogs,
And occasionally frogs,
But mostly his puppy called Daniel.

EMMELINE

A rich old lady – Emmeline
Drove around in a purple limousine.
She knew that the colour
Was unlike any other
And was copied from a car magazine.

EMORY. SEE EMERY.

EMRYS

A young zoologist called Emrys
Was detailed to study the pteromys.[25]
But squirrel sort-of-things
That use skins not wings
Are not well designed to impress.

ENA

There was a fat girl called Ena
Who wished to become much leaner.
She just couldn't win;
She became so thin
That people declared they'd not seen her.

---

[25] Pteromys: a genus comprising the flying squirrels.

ENGLEBERT

> A horrid young man – Englebert,
> Did his very best to disconcert.
> He would burn your toast
> And give you scrag-end of roast
> Or flaunt an outrageous T-shirt.

ENID

> There was a young angler called Enid
> Who said she'd caught a fat sciaenid.[26]
> She was quite upset
> When told by the vet
> That it was merely an old scorpaenid.

ENOCH

> There was an ancient man called Enoch
> Who lived in a different epoch.
> His sense of direction
> Needed some correction
> When he got lost in old Antioch.

ERASMUS

> There was a young author – Erasmus,
> Who was asked to explain a chiasmus.[27]
> "He went to the sea,
> But back home went she."
> He spat out in words miasmous.

---

[26] Sciaenid: a type of fish.

[27] Chiasmus: an inversion in the order of words in the second of two parallel phrases.

ERIC

A curvaceous young man called Eric
Had a form which was really quite spheric.
At twenty and one
He weighed half a ton,
And had reached his climacteric.

ERICA

A disobedient young child called Erica
Just wanted to leave America.
She got on a plane,
And was off to Spain
Before her parents could check her.

ERLE

There was a young monk called Erle
Who found an enormous pearl.
He started to roister
Right there in the cloister
And went on a social whirl.

ERMINTRUDE

There was a bright girl – Ermintrude,
Who set the price for Brent crude.
But she displeased the city
When she tried to be witty,
And appeared on TV in the nude.

ERNEST

An immature youth called Ernest
Used to cause us not a little unrest.
He once gave a pearl,
To a very pretty girl
But she used it to feather her nest.

ERNESTINE

There was a young girl – Ernestine,
Who didn't want to be seen.
She was terribly shy
And would say, "Hullo, goodbye!"
I think she was missing a gene.

ERNIE

An athletic young man called Ernie
Took part in a rather odd tourney.
'Twas a sort of pentathlon
Plus a three-quarter marathon,
And a roundabout sort of a journey.

ESAU

A brother of Jacob called Esau
Used to live in the bibles of yore.
Being ever so hairy
He was terribly scary,
And they always showed him the door.

ESME

A fast young girl called Esme
Always did her best to impress me.
I escaped to Spain,
But she found me again –
She was always able to out-guess me.

ESTELLA

A brash young girl – Estella,
Was known as a very loud yeller.
At considerable risk
They made a compact disc,
Which turned out to be a bestseller.

ESTELLE

An intellectual young girl – Estelle,
Did everything rather well.
One day with her kit
She made an atom split.
And the last thing we heard was her yell.

ESTHER

There was a teenager called Esther
Whose mother always undressed her.
You might think it a treat
When done in the street,
But the police would always arrest her.

ETHEL

There was a wise woman called Ethel
Who left her job at the local bethel.[28]
She said it had got
The smell of dry rot.
And the owners could go to the devil.

ETHELBERT

There was a young monarch – Ethelbert,[29]
Who said he felt terribly hurt.
"I am King of Kent,
But I live in a tent
And my Bertha thinks I'm a flirt."

---

[28] Bethel: in this instance an old ship fitted as a place of worship for sailors.

[29] Ethelbert: King of Kent (c.552-616) and other regions. Married to Bertha. a Frankish princess.

ETHELIND

There was a young girl – Ethelind,
Whose mother liked soup ready-thinned.
It prevented her daughter
From adding some water
To factory-made stuff that was tinned.

ETHELRED

There once was a King Ethelred
About whom not much is said.
He once fought in vain
In a war with a Dane.
And was succeeded by brother Alfred.[30]

ETTA

A practical young girl called Etta
Let nothing at all upset her.
And by solid devotion
She earned her promotion.
And became a real go-getter.

EUAN (ALSO EWAN AND EWEN)

A hungry young man called Euan,
Said, "Okay chaps, what's brewin'?"
He went off in a huff
When they said, "Not enough,
It's just a scrag-end that we're stewin'."

EUGENE

There was a young tenor – Eugene,
Who sang 'Begin the Beguine'.
He'd start in C sharp,
Then pluck at his harp
While beating time on a tambourine.

---

[30] King Alfred was Ethelred's younger brother.

EUGENIA

There was a young starlet – Eugenia,
Who went off for some filming in Kenya.
But she didn't get far,
Being upstaged by the star,
Who said, "After all – I'm the senior."

EULALIA

A girl at the palace called Eulalia
Used to look after all the regalia.
She was asked to pay the cost
Of a tiara she lost,
But she escaped by fleeing to Australia.

EUNICE (ALSO UNICE)

There was a musician called Eunice,
Who was asked, "Do you know what that tune is?"
"Just play the refrain,
Once more. Then again.
I'll know it when it's worn off its newness."

EUSEBIUS

We had an old pal called Eusebius
Who collected piles of bathybius.[31]
He then gave it away,
In a friendly way
And said it was just for use by us.

EUSTACE

A lovesick young man called Eustace
Was hoping to experience Sue's kiss.
He managed a squeeze
From a girl named Louise
But his wooing was really useless.

---

[31] Bathybius: a substance on the bottom of the sea.

EUSTACIOUS

There was a young snob called Eustacious
Who was really not very gracious.
It was a terrible shame
That his wife was the same
And she was so ostentatious.

EUSTACIA

There was a young girl called Eustacia
Who climbed up a thorny acacia.
She got very hot
And said, "I'm a clot.
Next time I'll go scale a glacier."

EVADNE

A very brave model called Evadne
Was doing an ad with a bad knee.
But when they asked for more,
She said, "There's the door
I think you'd better just fade me."

EVAN

A fussy old man called Evan
Always took his tea at eleven.
He said, "I don't care
If my wife is not here,
For she stops me having cream from Devon."

EVANGELINE

There was a young girl – Evangeline,
Who said, "I do like my name, it's fine.
I can pronounce it three ways,
Which I do on dull days,
And I can end it 'lin', 'leen' or 'line'."

EVE

A cheating young girl called Eve
Did her very best to deceive.
It was quite a big fib
To say she came from a rib,
And I just had to ask her to leave.

EVELINA

There was an old girl – Evelina,
Who was a very experienced convener.
But she grew autocratic
And a trifle dogmatic,
And became known as an intervener.

EVELYN

A haemophilic young girl called Evelyn
Once pricked herself with a pin.
Soon her lifeblood
Poured out in a flood
And she got quite noticeably thin.

EVELYN

Said a very young man called Evelyn
"I've just had a very strong gin.
It's gone to my head,
Please put me to bed,
But first shoot that pink zeppelin."

EVERARD

A poker-playing man – Everard,
Was covered all over with lard.
When we asked the explanation
For his body contamination,
He said it was for palming one card.

EVITA

A dictatorial young girl called Evita
Found no one was able to defeat her.
She would take people's wages
At once, or by stages.
Then stop them trying to unseat her.

EWAN. SEE EUAN.

EWART

There was an old painter called Ewart
Who studied the subject of zoo art.
He painted brown bears
With cross-eyed stares,
And implied that this was just true art.

EWEN. SEE EUAN.

EZEKIEL

There was an old angler – Ezekiel,
Who used to go out with his sea creel.
He would look for dab,
And the occasional crab
But he never went off to seek eel.

EZRA

There once was a rock 'n' roller called Ezra
Who had a short course with old Mesmer.
When staying in France,
He was put in a trance
And jived all the way to Andrezra.

F

A brilliant professor called Felix...

FABIAN

An ancient explorer called Fabian
Met up with an eccentric old Swabian.[32]
He said to the latter,
"It's of no matter,
But to me you look like an Arabian."

FAITH

A ghost of a girl called Faith
Appeared to be just like a wraith.
She was barely opaque,
And as thin as a rake;
In inches her waist was one eighth.

FANNY

There was a clairvoyant called Fanny,
A friend of my great aunt Annie.
She said, "You had tea
At a quarter past three."
Her knowledge was really uncanny.

FARAH (ALSO FARRAH)

A crazy young girl called Farah
Had attitudes that were always bizarre.
She'd say, "Want a ride?
Well, just get inside!"
But quickly drive off in her car.

FAUSTINA

A jealous young girl called Faustina
Did her very best to oust Tina.
Tina was her lodger
Who made eyes at Roger.
But he only had time for Gina.

---

[32] Swabian: an inhabitant of Swabia which was a duchy of south-west Germany from 1079-1268.

FAUSTINE

A girl at an auction – Faustine,
Won a bid for an old magazine.
When she saw the ammunition
In her new acquisition,
It turned her a bright shade of green.

FAWN

A party-going girl called Fawn
Went and opened her window at dawn.
When she had climbed back in,
She drank a large gin,
Which she had just redeemed from pawn.

FAY (ALSO FAYE)

There was a young girl called Fay
Who went off to work on a sleigh.
She controlled her horse
By orders in Morse,
Which replied with a yea or a neigh.

FELICE

A lovesick young girl called Felice
Had a boyfriend in the police.
She'd dial 999
And say, "I am thine."
But got arrested for disturbing the peace.

FELICIA

A pretty young girl called Felicia
Had lips that I declare were kissier
Than others I've known
When we were alone,
But the boys just think I am sissier.

FELICITY

A go-getting girl called Felicity
Was known for her eccentricity.
To bring to fruition
Her cherished ambition
She used some bizarre publicity.

FELIX

A brilliant professor called Felix
Designed a robot-like helix.
It would add or deduct
And then self-destruct,
But rise up again like a phoenix.

FENELLA

A strange young girl called Fenella
Always used an antique umbrella.
When out in the rain,
She looked quite inane,
But no one wanted to tell her.

FERDINAND

An old ornithologist – Ferdinand,
Often held a young bird in hand.
One sat on his sleeve
Disinclined to leave,
Then swallowed his wedding band.

FERNANDO

There was a pianist called Fernando
Who decided to become a commando.
But he failed the course
When his sergeant got hoarse
Forbidding him to march *rallentando*.

FFION (PRONOUNCED FEE-ON)

> A rich young girl called Ffion
> Had her own piste to ski on.
> When I saw her slalom,
> I could see future stardom.
> Which I and her friends all agree on.

FIDEL

> There was a rude man called Fidel
> Who gave everyone the needle.
> Here I recommend
> That you stress the end,
> And not the start or the middle.

FIFI

> A modern young girl called Fifi
> Made out she was ever so chichi.[33]
> What a pity her face
> Lacked symmetry and grace,
> And her figure was wide and so beefy.

FILIPA

> Said a young girl called Filipa,
> "I'm afraid that I have a silly pa."
> They replied, "So we're agreed,
> For he washes in mead,
> Then tries to straighten his scimitar."

FINGAL

> A young misogynist called Fingal
> Was quite loath to intermingle.
> No need to mention
> His avowed intention
> Of remaining completely single.

---

[33] Chichi: in this connection – stylish.

FIONA

A neat little girl called Fiona
Dwelt alone on the Isle of Iona.
Her cottage was so clean
It could be called pristine.
"After all," she said, "I'm the owner."

FITZROY

A spiteful young man called Fitzroy
Went out of his way to annoy.
He'd switch off the telly,
Hide just one wellie,
Or ruin a favourite toy.

FLAVIA

There was a old woman called Flavia
With the most outrageous behaviour.
She'd dance a jig
On the back of a pig.
Then go to a ball in Belgravia.

FLEUR

There was a bashful girl called Fleur
Who covered herself with myrrh.[34]
When I asked her why,
She said, "'Cos I'm shy,
And I stick to what I prefer."

FLO

An ambitious young girl called Flo
Said that her life was all go.
When they cried, "Slow down!"
She'd just give a frown;
But she stopped when I just shouted, "Whoa!"

---

[34] Myrrh: an aromatic gum.

FLOELLA

There was a young skater – Floella
Who always put up her umbrella.
She said that the thrust
From the occasional gust
Pulled her along just like a propeller.

FLORA

There was an old woman called Flora
Who was known as the world's worst snorer.
When a bull heard her snort
'Twas a rival it thought,
And went out of its way to gore her.

FLORENCE

A scantily dressed girl called Florence
Looked up at the sky with abhorrence.
She said the forecaster
Was an absolute disaster
As the rain came down in torrents.

FLOY

A keen archaeologist called Floy
Went off to find ancient Troy.
She couldn't afford a liner
To take her to Asia Minor
So she sailed all the way in a hoy.

FLOYD

There was a young spaceman called Floyd
Who landed on an asteroid,
But he found the g
Was only point 003
And his first step shot him into the void.

FRAN

A dotty young girl called Fran
Had a date for a new body scan.
They searched in vain
For a sign of a brain,
Which wasn't part of their plan.

FRANCES

A new sequence dancer called Frances
Receives some curious glances.
We all take a risk
When she does a whisk
For she doesn't know where the line-of-dance is.

FRANCESCA

There was a young girl called Francesca
Who decided to live in Briviesca.
She sailed off in her boat
Wearing just a fur coat,
With a crew of one cook and a lascar.

FRANCIE

A gambling fanatic called Francie
Made wagers that were always so chancy.
She never won a bet
At games like roulette
Which did nothing to ever entrance me.

FRANCINE

A fierce young girl called Francine
Was always creating a scene.
When she gave me a clout,
I let out a shout,
"I think your behaviour's obscene."

FRANCIS

Said a young rider called Francis,
"My horse is the one that prances.
He does other things too,
Such as throwing a shoe,
And giving me wicked glances."

FRANK

There was an old man called Frank
Who had his very own bank.
It wasn't his fault
He got locked in the vault
When the door shut fast with a clank.

FRANKIE

A queer-looking man called Frankie
Had a nose that was long, thin and lanky.
He once got cross
And why? 'Twas because
He'd lost his extra-long hankie.

FRASIER

They said of a conjurer called Frasier
That there really is no one crazier.
His presdigitation
Astounded the nation,
And his card tricks would really amaze yer.

FRED

There was a young scrounger called Fred
Who would never get out of bed.
I said, "Put on your shirt,
And try to find work!"
He replied, "Up with you I am fed!"

FREDA (ALSO FRIEDA)

There was a girl farmer called Freda
Who worked as a pure calf-breeder.
She worked to rule
Until an irate bull
Tossed her up and into the feeder.

FREDDIE

An immature man we called Freddie
Never ever seemed to be ready.
When he reached twenty-nine
He was offered some wine,
But he preferred to play with his teddy.

FREDERIC (ALSO FREDERICK)

There was an old farmer called Frederic
Who bought a new house with redder brick.
He then went away
To help make hay
And with ideas for making a better rick.

FREDERICA

There was a queer girl called Frederica.
If you wish to see her, first seek her.
And just a reminder
That when you find her,
She likes you to shout, "Eureka!"

FRIEDA. SEE FREDA.

FRITZ

There was a clever man called Fritz
Who lived by the use of his wits.
It was his intention
To save for a pension.
Then he would just call it quits.

FULLER

There was a young cleric called Fuller
Who was the one who applied the bulla.[35]
Not knowing the score,
He caused a war
When an edict was sent to a mullah.

---

[35] Bulla: the seal on a papal bull.

G

There once was a chef called Godfrey...

GABBY (ALSO GABI)

> A lazy young man called Gabby
> Had employment in Abu Dhabi.
> He disliked the toil
> Of working in oil
> So instead got a job as a cabby.

GABBY (ALSO GABI)

> A hair-brained young girl called Gabby
> Used to do naughty things in the abbey.
> She once sold shampoo
> From the back of a pew.
> Then told the priest he looked shabby.

GABRIEL

> There was a man called Gabriel,
> Who said, "Was this guy Abe real?"
> I said, "The answer's yes,
> He had the right address,
> Which gave him a certain appeal."

GABRIELLE

> There was a bright girl – Gabrielle
> Who was quite a young demoiselle.
> She said geologically,
> Or philosophically,
> Life was a mere bagatelle.

GAIL (ALSO GALE)

> An athletic young man called Gail
> Used to run ten miles a day without fail.
> When out on the flat
> He'd beat Postman Pat,
> So they used him to deliver the mail.

GALE

There was a young girl called Gale
Who always went around in a veil.
When they asked her why,
She said, "'Twas to try
To deter a certain young male."

GARETH

There was a young soldier called Gareth
Who daily faced wounding or death.
He destroyed a tank
Getting near his flank
In the desert battle of Mareth.[36]

GARFIELD

The son of a farmer called Garfield
Worked all by himself in a far field.
He also made shoes
For tame kangaroos;
He did the sewing while Pa heeled.

GARLAND

There was a young rambler called Garland
Who got tired of doing what Ma planned.
To be free to roam
He left his old home
And went to a distant and far land.

GARRY

There was a young widower called Garry
Who started a new Cash and Carry.
He said, "The hours I keep
Would ruin a wife's sleep.
So I'd better not plan to remarry."

---

[36] Mareth: a battle of World War II.

GARTH

A blaspheming old man called Garth
Was easily aroused to wrath.
I'm glad I wasn't there
When he started to swear,
That day he fell in the hearth.

GAVIN

There was a young rider called Gavin
Whose horse had suffered from spavin.[37]
He took his old hack
To a local quack,
Who said he'd rub it with savin.[38]

GAWAIN

A gigolo, they said, was Gawain
Who was inclined to be somewhat vain.
He took particular care
With his long curly hair
Which he wrapped up in black Cellophane.

GAY (ALSO GAYE)

There was a young lady called Gay,
A name not much used today.
When they changed the meaning,
It was most demeaning
For all the girls they betray.

---

[37] Spavin: a disease of the hock joint of horses.

[38] Savin: a species of juniper.

GAYLE

A miser of a man was Gayle
Who carried his cash in a pail.
He sailed from Nantucket
With a very full bucket,
But he sank in a force eight gale.

GAYLE

A spendthrift young girl called Gayle
Went alone to a car boot sale.
She was much too rash,
And spent her cash
On two dead hens and a quail.

GAYLORD (ALSO GAYLORDE)

A debonair young man called Gaylord
Was steely-eyed and square-jawed.
His life was not soothing
For he was fast-moving
And travelled the world by Concorde.

GEENA (ALSO GINA)

There was a fat redhead called Geena
Who jumped into a Spanish arena.
As she ran round the ring
She learnt one good thing:
It's a good way to make yourself leaner.

GEMMA

There was a young girl called Gemma
Who rose at five ack emma.[39]
She'd drive off to war,
In those days of yore
And reduce the manpower dilemma.

---

[39] Ack emma: an old alphabetical code for a.m.

GENE (ALSO JEAN)

A university student called Gene
Once ran out of gasoline.
She arrived too late
At the campus gate
To take her Latin Unseen.[40]

GENE

A nosy young man called Gene
Always tended to intervene.
One hot summer's day
He spied an affray.
And now he's a might-have-been.

GEOF (ALSO GEOFF)

There was a young man called Geof,
Who asked, "What is meant by a clef?"
I said, "In a musical score…"
But he cried, "No more!
I must tell you that I am tone deaf."

GEOFFREY

An English student – Geoffrey
Once asked what was meant by re.
I said, "Re your remark
I will now make a start,
There are four meanings. Now let me see…"

GEORGE

There was a fat blacksmith called George
Who worked in his grandfather's forge.
He'd cook his meal
On a hot piece of steel
Then sit on the anvil and gorge.

---

[40] Latin Unseen: a type of school examination.

GEORGETTE

A strange young girl was Georgette,
She ate beans, but not courgettes.
She swore mighty oaths
And wore colourful clothes,
But on Sundays she always wore jet.

GEORGIA

A girl at my school called Georgia
Was a descendant of Lucrezia Borgia.
Her nicknames were many –
Some called her Genny.
Others called her Georgy, or Gia.

GEORGIANA

An equestrian girl – Georgiana,
Used to hail from Lousiana.
She fell off her horse
Right into some gorse
Whilst riding in the local gymkhana.

GEORGIANA (WHEN PRONOUNCED GEORGE- AYNA)

There was an eccentric girl – Georgiana,
And there couldn't be anyone vainer.
She spent long hours
In hot and cold showers;
In the end we had to restrain her.

GEORGINA

A girl of many parts was Georgina,
She'd mix jam with semolina.
Then eat it with a spoon,
Whilst playing a bassoon
And the base of a concertina.

GERAINT

Pronounce 'ain't' as 'eye-nt'.

> There was a man in a pub called Geraint
> Who always drank just half a pint.
> That was enough
> To make him get rough,
> For a gentleman he certainly ain't.

GERALD

> There was a young prince called Gerald
> Who got out of bed and then yelled:
> "Page! Don't stay lurking,
> Bring along my jerkin!
> Then send for the duty herald!"

GERALDINE

> A rich young girl – Geraldine,
> Used to own a large limousine.
> She found it too much
> For her feminine touch,
> So, instead, bought a sewing machine.

GERARD (ALSO JERRARD)

> A lounge lizard type called Gerard
> From every fine club was barred.
> He tried a disguise
> And one or two lies
> Then found himself feathered and tarred.

GERDA

> A veiled foreign girl called Gerda
> Was by custom always in purdah.
> She cried, "Let me out!
> Or I'll call a boy scout,
> And for me I'm sure he'll do murder."

GERMAN

I once knew a scruff called German
Whose nickname at school was just Herman.
Now, can that be him,
Standing neat and trim,
In the pulpit preaching a sermon?

GERMAINE

A beautiful girl called Germaine
Always used to drive me insane.
I asked for a date,
But I had a long wait,
For I never once saw her again.

GERRIE (ALSO GERRY AND JERRY)

There was a young sailor called Gerrie
Who built a light plastic wherry.[41]
He put in a wheel
Of heavy-grade steel,
But the boat capsized near the ferry.

GERT

There was a young girl called Gert
Who always seemed frightfully pert.
It came as a blow,
When I told her so
And she said she was terribly hurt.

GERTIE

There once was a woman called Gertie
Who always seemed terribly dirty.
She had many wrinkles
And lines and crinkles,
Which made her look forty not thirty.

---

[41] Wherry: a light shallow boat, sharp at both ends.

GERVAISE

A loquacious young girl – Gervaise,
Tried to master the paraphrase.
She once had to shorten
A speech for Charles Laughton
And received from him nothing but praise.

GERVASE

A slave to drugs was Gervase
And he had most peculiar ways.
He'd breath in some "ice"
Mixed up with some spice,
Then walk around in a daze.

GHISLAINE

A keen young pilot was Ghislaine
Who possessed her own aeroplane.
She once tried to drink soup
At the top of a loop,
But found the knack much too arcane

GIDEON

There was an old scientist called Gideon
Famous for his work with obsidian.
But he always sought
The longitude nought,
And the line of the Greenwich meridian.

GIL (ALSO GILL)

A foppish young man called Gil
Always wore ties made of twill.
That was okay by me
Till he came out to tea
Wearing a tricorn hat with a frill.

GILBERT

I once met a man called Gilbert
Who, one might say, was ill girt.
I wondered why
He had a collar and tie
That were not attached to his shirt.

GILES (ALSO GYLES)

A lame young man called Giles
Would ramble for miles and miles.
His pace was quite brisk,
But he took a big risk
When he tried to jump over stiles.

GILL. SEE GIL.

GILLIAN (ALSO JILLIAN)

There was a young woman called Gillian
Who went for a ride on a pillion.
She could see nothing but hair,
Which grew here and there,
And was streaked in blue and vermilion.

GILLIE (ALSO GILLY AND JILLY)

A wee Scottish lassie called Gillie
Lived where the land was quite hilly.
One day by a loch
She met Ludwig Koch[42]
Recording his bird-song willy-nilly.

GINA. SEE GEENA.

---

[42] Ludwig Koch: a pioneer of recording and interpreting bird-song.

GINETTE

An adventurous young girl called Ginette
Once climbed on her roof for a bet.
She achieved some renown
When she couldn't get down –
What she did in the end I forget.

GINGER

There was an old man called Ginger
Who went out of his way to injure.
He'd cast an aspersion
On most every person.
And in my case he called me a whinger.

GINNY

There was a new driver called Ginny
Who said, "I'm a bit of a ninny.
To be quite candid,
Here I am stranded,
In the country by my rusty old mini."

GINTY

A greedy old lady called Ginty
Liked all her sweets strong and minty.
I once had a shock
When I gave her a choc.
For her eyes went all hard and flinty.

GISELLE

An animal lover called Giselle
Used to keep a tame old gazelle.
We said, "It's quite sweet,
And has such pretty feet
But we cannot put up with the smell."

GLAD

A friendless young spinster called Glad
Had replies from a lonely hearts ad.
On the first occasion,
She formed a liaison,
Then found the man was a cad.

GLADYS

There was a young golfer called Gladys
Who said, "I know my looks are like Daddy's.
I may seem quite plain
But I have Mum's brain,
And my putting's as good as my caddie's."

GLENDA

There was an old soak called Glenda
Who often went out on a bender.
With an old half a crown
She'd go out on the town,
But she never had legal tender.

GLORIA

An excitable girl called Gloria
Always lived in a state of euphoria.
She said it was no fun
To live like a nun,
Or to emulate Queen Victoria.

GLYN (ALSO GLYNN)

There was an old man called Glyn
Who was married to a Bedouin.
His son, like his dad,
Became a nomad,
And always used the prefix of 'Bin'.

GODFREY

There once was a chef called Godfrey
Who was able to get his cod free.
It was cooked in the refectory
By the local rectory
Then served on a salver to the godly.

GODWIN

There was a young Rocker[43] called Godwin
Who said, "Don't let that nasty Mod win;
He is a live wire,
But he's also a liar,
To do so would be an odd sin."

GORDON

There was a young Arab called Gordon
Who lived quite near Ma'an in Jordan.
He had a job in Petra
And other places, et cetera,
As the senior road traffic warden.

GORE

There was a young cowboy called Gore
Who married an Indian squaw.
They had a papoose,
Two hens and a goose
And a rather loquacious macaw.

---

[43] Rocker: a member of the teenage motor cycling gangs of the 1960s who wore leather jackets and were rivals to the Mods who wore neat clothes.

GRACE

There was a young sailor called Grace
Who entered the Fastnet race.
She was quite alarmed
On becoming becalmed,
And was outrun by a couple of plaice.

GRACIE

There was a brash girl called Gracie
Whose clothes were exquisitely lacy.
She made no concessions
To anyone's impressions;
Her thoughts were distinctly racy.

GRAHAM

The next verse should be read with an American accent and in the dialect that tends to make a single syllable word into a two-syllable word. Thus Damn and Ma'am become "Day-am" and "May-yam".

An offensive young man called Graham
Stubbed his big toe and cried, "Damn!"
My wife said, "I don't care
To hear people swear."
To which he replied, "So sorry Ma'am!"

GRAEME

There was a young chemist called Graeme
Who had only himself to blame.
His drink was too flaccid
So he added some acid,
And his widow won the insurance claim.

GRANVILLE

There was a young smith called Granville
Who smashed his foot on an anvil.
"We mustn't delay it,"
They said. "We'll X-ray it
If that won't help, then a scan will."

GREG

There was a young lad called Greg
Who wanted to hatch out an egg.
But he got very scared
When a chick appeared
And took a good peck at his leg.

GREGORY

There was a new farmhand called Gregory
Who got a good job in an eggery.
It was just too much,
When he stole a clutch,
And now he just resorts to beggery.

GRESHAM

There was a young farmer called Gresham
Who bought cogs and tried to mesh 'em.
There was fascination
With his explanation:
"Those sheaves – it's so I can thresh 'em."

GRETA

A dashing young girl called Greta
Once said, "I've never felt better.
I've won the pools,
I'm finished with fools
And now I'll become a jetsetter."

GRETCHEN

There was a young girl called Gretchen
Whose job was carryin' and fetchin'.
But her life was changed
When she arranged
To take up a course in sketchin'.

GREVILLE

There was a young pilot called Greville
Who was told to fly straight and level.
He said, "Don't be a loon,
This thing's a balloon,
And maintaining height is the devil."

GRIFF

There was an old priest called Griff
Who walked on the edge of a cliff.
As they said, "Come on down."
He tripped on his gown,
And screamed, "Yes, I won't be a jiff!"

GRIFFITH

There was an old man called Griffith
Who lisped when he talked to his miffif.
'Twas the same when he wrote,
From all places remote
He'd omit the s in his miffive.

GRISELL (ALSO GRISSEL, GRIZEL, AND GRIZZEL)

The manager of our shop called Grisell
Always vets the items we sell.
The meat might look tough,
Or the pies seem rough,
But she'd judge them all by the smell.

GUINEVERE

There was a young girl – Guinevere,
Who went off to a film première.
When she told the film hero
His rating was zero,
He replied, "In that case we make a good pair."

GUS

There was a young student called Gus,
Who said, "I can't live with a fuss.
My sums might be wrong,
I draw squares oblong,
And I don't know minus from plus."

GUSTUS

There once was a man called Gustus,
Which is a diminutive of Augustus.
He was also a crook,
And when brought to book,
You should have heard how he cussed us!

GUY

There was a young man called Guy,
Who said that he wanted to fly.
He would flap some fans
Attached to his hands –
Well… at least he had a good try.

GWEN

An insatiable girl called Gwen
Said she had a bit of a yen.
"I know I'm barmy,
But I'd like some salami
And served on a plate in my den."

GWENDOLEN

Said a young girl – Gwendolen,
"My name's not pronounced len but lin.
I know it is hard
For a prospective bard
But it's a matter of discipline."

GWENNIE

There was an old woman called Gwennie
Who used to drink one too many.
But rampant inflation
Reduced her libation
For beer now costs more than a penny.

GWILLYM (ALSO GWILYM)

Said a young army recruit called Gwillym,
"That sergeant major – I'll kill 'im!
He told Corp on parade
I don't make the grade,
'So get hold of Gwillym and drill 'im.'"

GWYNETH

In olden-day language young Gwyneth
Is one of the people who sinneth.
But she is good in parts,
And at the game of darts
She is always the one who winneth!

GYLES. SEE GILES.

H

There was a young Viking called Hayden...

HABBIE

There was a young Scot called Habbie
Who knew all the works of Rabbie.[44]
He'd recite them aloud
To an admiring crowd,
Or, if alone, to his tabby.

HADRIAN

Publius Aelius Hadrian[45]
Was a Spaniard adopted by Trajan.
He once built a wall
Just ten feet tall,
And retired a rich Arcadian.

HAL

A new young barrister called Hal
Defended a crook at a trial.
He was held in contempt
For being unkempt
And addressing the judge as Old Gal.

HAMISH

There was a fierce Scot called Hamish
Whose godmother gave him one wish.
He said, "Give me some pipes
With some tartan stripes,
And a sporran that's definitely clannish."

---

[44] Rabbie: Robert Burns, Scottish poet, 1759-1796.

[45] Hadrian: full name Publius Aelius Hadrianus; Roman emperor, AD 76-138.

HANK

A young man from New York called Hank
Once said, "You can tell I'm a Yank.
I roll my Rs
Own two large cars,
And have one million bucks in the bank."

HANS

A young investor called Hans
Had many ambitious plans.
He would buy out some firms
On outrageous terms,
Then give them away to his fans.

HARALD (ALSO HAROLD)

At Christmas a pilot called Harald
Carried out a roll which he barrelled.[46]
The roll was quite neat,
So he was held in his seat,
And as he flew by he carolled.

HARDI (ALSO HARDY)

There was a young soldier called Hardi
Who was called out to fight the Mahdi.[47]
With his camel on strike
He arrived on his bike,
But the Captain complained he was tardy.

---

[46] Barrelled, i.e. he did a barrel roll so was held in his seat by centrifugal force.

[47] Mahdi: in this case, the Moslem leader Mohammed Ahmed who captured Khartoum in 1885.

HARLEY

There was a young farmer called Harley
Who said, "I'm a proper old Charlie,
I've got in the wheat
For us all to eat,
But I've quite forgotten the barley."

HARRIET (ALSO HARIETTE AND HARRIOT)

There was a Roman bride called Harriet
Who wanted to arrive in her chariot.
It was quite a shame
When her horse went lame,
But she was rescued by Judas Iscariot.

HARRISON

There was a young private called Harrison
Who was stationed at the local garrison.
He was handsome and tall
And if that is not all,
He was better than Apollo by comparison.

HARRY

There was a large man called Harry
Who intended to ride in a gharry.[48]
But the driver said, "No,
It is just no go,
A small man is all I can carry."

HARVEY

There was a young angler called Harvey
Who bought half a kilo of larvae.
He just couldn't wait
To use some as bait,
But all he could catch was one garvie.[49]

---

[48] Gharry: an Indian wheeled vehicle.
[49] Garvie: a sprat.

HATTY

There was an old girl called Hatty
Who everyone said was quite scatty.
They also said her donkey
Looked ever so wonky,
But I think they were just being catty.

HAYDEN

There was a young Viking called Hayden
Who met a beautiful maiden.
He removed her of course,
To the land of the Norse,
But that's what you do when you're raidin'.

HAYLEY

There was a charlady called Hayley
Who worked as my old aunt's "daily".
Her taking ways
Were a passing phase,
But she found herself in the Old Bailey.

HAZEL

There was an aspiring singer called Hazel
Who went for a test and appraisal.
But they said her high C
Was more like a B,
And her vowels were really too nasal.

HEATHER

There was a young girl called Heather
Who always wore clothes made of leather.
One day in her haste
Her blouse came unlaced,
And she exposed pink flesh to the weather.

HECTOR

There was a young bobby called Hector
Who became a police inspector.
He had swift promotion
Due to devotion
And his skill as a crime detector.

HEDDA

There was a young cook called Hedda
Who bought a new garden shredder.
She put in some curds,
Said a few words,
And produced a pound of ripe cheddar.

HEIDI

There was a young girl called Heidi
Who never kept anything tidy.
Her house was a mess,
And as for her dress…!
But then, as she said, "I'm no lidy!"

HELEN

There was a Scots lass called Helen
Who walked by a loch and fell in.
She had quite a soak,
Couldn't swim a stroke,
So thought she'd better start yellin'.

HELENA

There was a young child called Helena
Who some people said had the hell in her.
But others who met her
Seemed to know better
And said it was only the gel in her.

HELGA

A mysterious girl called Helga
Was wont at times to yell, "Gar!"
She might be a bit dishy
But to me it sounds fishy,
Or perhaps she might just be gaga.

HELOISE

A greedy young girl called Heloise
Grew much too fond of her mellow cheese.
She'd keep it in store,
With a lock on the door
Wrapped up in her yellow chemise.

HENRIETTA

There was a skilled pianist – Henrietta
Who could play a brisk arietta.
And she would dote
On songs from Showboat
And one from Naughty Marietta.

HENRY

There was a chicken farmer called Henry
Who lived on the island of Zendry.
A hole in the fence
Left him no defence,
And a fox ran free in the hennery.

HERB

An uncultured man called Herb
Knew not a noun from a verb.
But despite the wordy muddle,
The girls gave him a cuddle,
For the size of his smile was superb.

HERMAN

There was a young Russian called Herman
Who got trapped in a treacherous urman.[50]
He managed to get free
By grabbing a tree,
And being helped by a passing German.

HERMIONE

I worked for a girl called Hermione
Who said she could always rely on me.
Her clientele grew,
From nought to a few
In her business of growing white briony.

HESTER

There was a sloppy girl called Hester
Who shopped in a yellow sou'wester.
I said, "It looks nice,
But take my advice,
That is not the fashion in Chester."

HETTY

There was an old tourist called Hetty
Who said she once saw a yeti.
But without any ado,
We knew this was untrue,
For she claimed it was eating spaghetti.

HEW (ALSO HEWE, HUGH AND HUW)

There was a strange man called Hew
Who suddenly started to mew.
Not only that,
He purred like our cat,
So they put him away in a zoo.

---

[50] Urman: a swampy pine forest in Russia.

HEZEKIAH

There was a young man – Hezekiah,
Who wanted to become a good flier.
His mother said, "Go!
But always fly slow,
At one hundred feet and no higher.

HILARY (ALSO HILLARY)

A young businesswoman called Hilary
Possessed her very own distillery.
She would sell direct
To the more select,
Such as the Royal Artillery.

HILDA

There was a young soldier called Hilda
Who used to sing whenever they drilled her.
When her sergeant heard,
He fought for a word,
Then used language that really chilled her.

HILLARY. SEE HILARY.

HIRAM (ALSO HYRAM)

There was an old employer called Hiram
Who would hire some hands and then fire 'em.
When I said, "Don't they swear?"
He replied, "Loud and clear,
But you've really got to admire 'em!"

HOBBIE

There was an MP called Hobbie
Who was arrested one day in the lobby.
He shouted out, "Damn!
Don't you know who I am?"
But was taken away by a bobby.

HOLLY

I had an old aunt called Holly
Who was brash and so frightfully jolly.
When she slapped your back
You felt something crack,
And she never ever said sorry.

HOMER

There was an old poet called Homer,
Who told about Odysseus the roamer.
He said he used gel
Which held his hair well
But was not too keen on the aroma.

HONEY

There was an old woman called Honey
Whom everyone thought looked funny.
After winning the lottery
She had a lobotomy,
Which utilised most of her money.

HONOR

There was a teenager called Honor
Who thought she'd drink belladonna.
She realised her fate
A minute too late
And collapsed saying, "Gosh, I'm a goner!"

HONORIA

There was a young girl called Honoria
Who fell into an old type of noria.[51]
She said as it spun,
"I find this quite fun!"
Then passed out in a fit of euphoria.

---

[51] Noria: a water wheel that discharges water into a trough as it revolves.

HONORIOUS

A bit of a crook was Honorious
Whose career was not at all glorious.
He would sell his drugs
To idiots and mugs.
And became so very notorious.

HOPE

A filthy old man called Hope
Always abhorred the use of soap.
And come what may,
Men would keep away,
For he reeked like dirty old rope.

HORACE

An animal lover called Horace
Went off to buy a pet loris.[52]
It was quite a sight
To see it each night
Riding on top of his Morris.

HORATIO

A mathematician called Horatio
Once found an odd-shaped pistachio.
He said, "Oh my!
I'll have to use pi
To work out the right sort of ratio."

HORTENSE

There was a young shopper – Hortense,
Who kept long queues in suspense.
People would curse,
As she searched in her purse
For the exact amount of the pence.

---

[52] Loris: an Asiatic lemur.

HORTENSIA

There was a very shy girl, Hortensia
Who belonged to the intelligentsia.
But her father's edict
Was really quite strict,
And he'd never let any gent see her.

HOWARD

There was a bright diplomat called Howard
Who with plenary control was empowered.
He found diplomacy paid,
When he said, "Don't invade."
So relations with others weren't soured.

HOWIE

There was a young pilot called Howie
Who set off in his glider from Douai.
With lots of lift
He made short shift
Of the great circle route to Maui.

HUBERT

There was a young soldier – Hubert,
Who said he was going to desert.
But some little birds
Heard all of his words
And the guards were put on alert.

HUGH. SEE HEW.

HUGHIE

There was a young "Kiwi"[53] called Hughie
Who tried to get close to a tui.[54]
The bird went back
As he crept down a track,
And flew off when he yodelled, "Cooee!"

HUGO

A young mountaineer called Hugo
Once climbed up a hill where few go.
He was quite agog,
When down came a fog,
And cried, "Where did that lovely view go?"

HULDA (ALSO HULDAH)

There was a daring girl called Hulda
Whose clothes got louder and louder.
And not only this,
When I gave her a kiss,
My face became covered with powder.

HUMBERT

Said a very young boy called Humbert,
"This is what makes my thumb hurt:
Divide a metre by a chain.
Then do it again!
When I try it my brain goes numb, Bert."

---

[53] Kiwi: slang for a New Zealander.

[54] Tui: a New Zealand bird.

HUMPHREY (ALSO HUMPHRY)

A hedonistic young man called Humphrey
Said, "This sofa really ain't lump-free."
With a lot of pushin'
He threw out a cushion,
Which was one way to make himself comfy.

HUW. SEE HEW.

HYACINTH

A hardware store girl – Hyacinth,
Used to mix up her paints on a plinth.
To pay for her SERPS[55]
She'd distil out some turps,
Which she got from a tall terebinth.[56]

HYRAM. SEE HIRAM.

HY

A New Zealander from Dunedin called Hy
Would greet me by saying, "Haeremai!"[57]
He'd then strike some poses
And make me rub noses;
He'd do the same when we said good-bye.

HYWEL (ALSO HYWELL)

There was as young pilot called Hywel
Who was known to be able to fly well.
He'd often drink a gin
While doing a spin.
At that rate, they said he would die well.

---

[55] SERPS: State Earnings-Related Pension Scheme.

[56] Terebinth: the turpentine tree.

[57] Haeremai: Maori for "welcome".

I

A potential young flier called Icarus...

IAIN (ALSO IAN)

There was an old Red called Iain
Whose outlook was distinctly plebeian.
He was heard to mutter
How he was born in the gutter,
But claimed to have known Brenden Behan.

ICARUS

A potential young flier called Icarus
Told me he was heartily sick of us.
He would get away
By air some day,
But we all thought him rather ridiculous.

IDA

There was a young sailor called Ida
Who had only a compass to guide her.
She hit some rocks
On the way to the docks,
And wished that the channel were wider.

IDRIS

There was an old king called Idris
Who said, "Now listen you all, dig this!
I've found my crown
Has been painted light brown.
And I think the culprit was Swiss."

IFOR

There was a young sailor called Ifor
Who always aimed for the lee shore.
He would give an ETA[58]
From quite far away,
But would always arrive just before.

---

[58] ETA: Estimated Time of Arrival.

IGNACIO

There was a young prince called Ignacio
Who lived in a very large palacio.
It was four times as long
As a Gershwin song –
So now you can work out the ratio.

IGNATIUS

A boastful young man called Ignatius
Said he lived in quarters quite spacious.
He referred to small rooms
As a place for his brooms
But he always was terribly mendacious.

IGOR

There was a young farmer called Igor
Who couldn't believe what he saw:
His favourite pig
Was doing a jig,
And dancing around with a boar.

ILENA

There was a young artiste called Ilena
Who was a very good entertainer.
She could dance and sing
And do anything
That would pay the rent and sustain her.

ILONA

There was a young witch called Ilona
Who said she would be a blood donor.
But they found in her vein
Just the essence of bane;
So, with tact, they said they would phone her.

IMELDA

A young artisan called Imelda
Was employed on a ship as a welder.
But the top of the mast
Was swaying so fast
She could only do the job if they held her.

IMMANUEL. SEE EMMANUEL.

IMOGEN

There was a young girl – Imogen,[59]
Whose name was once Innogen.
Or it was until
The bard, with his quill,
Made a slip and joined up the n.

IMOGENE

There was dignified girl – Imogene
The one with two Es I mean.
In the family tradition
She had great ambition,
And thought she'd make a good queen.

INES (ALSO INEZ AND INNES)

A poker-playing girl called Ines
Could always come up with an ace.
Having concealed it
She'd suddenly reveal it.
But always kept a very straight face.

---

[59] Imogen: originally Innogen, but alleged to be a slip by Shakespeare when writing *Cymbeline*.

IONA

An imaginative girl called Iona
Remarked, "I've just dreamt of Pomona.[60]
And I was told
To be warlike and bold."
But I told her she meant Bellona.[61]

IRENA

There was a young athlete called Irena
Who always ran around in one trainer.
On one leg she'd hop.
Then do a quick swap;
There was nothing I could do to restrain her.

IRENE (ALSO EIRENE)

There was a young coquette called Irene
Who was always making a scene.
She once tried to flirt
With a boy named Bert,
But found he was not very keen.

IRIS

There was a young student called Iris
Who was keen to study the Maoris.
It was not too far
To the nearest pah,[62]
Where she started a series of diaries.

---

[60] Pomona: the Roman goddess of fruit trees.

[61] Bellona: the Roman goddess of war.

[62] Pah: a Maori settlement.

IRMA

There was a young explorer called Irma
Who trudged through the jungles of Burma.
She could cope with the heat
And bites on her feet,
But wished the going were firmer.

IRVING

There was a young waiter called Irving
Whose faults were quite unnerving.
He'd serve food cold
And was much too bold,
So they gave him more lessons in serving.

ISA

An impecunious young girl called Isa
Had thoughts about becoming a miser.
She had a bash
At hoarding her cash,
And completely ignored her adviser.

ISAAC (ALSO IZAAC)

A man who was all thumbs called Isaac
Once said, "I am taken aback,
I'm having a go
At trying to sew.
It's just that I can't find the knack."

ISABEL (ALSO ISOBEL AND ISABELLE)

A girl in a daze – Isabel,
Said, "Things are not going too well.
When I gaze around
From wall to the ground,
I find I've been put in a cell."

ISABELLA

There was a young girl – Isabella,
Who was painted by Sir Godfrey Kneller.
He tried to conceal
That last hearty meal
By posing her behind an umbrella.

ISABELLE. SEE ISABEL.

ISADOR (ALSO ISADORE)

A delicate young man – Isador
Once thought he could lay down the law.
But since he was effete,
And his height was five feet,
He usually got a sock on the jaw!

ISADORA

There was sad girl – Isadora,
Who said that boys would ignore her.
I told her that for passion
She should not follow fashion
And all the boys would adore her.

ISOBEL. SEE ISABEL.

ISOLD (ALSO ISOLDE)

There was a chilly girl called Isold
Who said, "I'm going to find gold.
But I won't go to Prussia,
Or even to Russia,
'Cos there it's too blooming cold."

ISOLDA

There was a nervous young girl called Isolda
Who always did what her mum told her.
That is, until
She met that man Bill,
And after that she got so much bolder.

ISRAEL

There was a young man called Israel
Who was once sent a bomb in his mail.
It was lucky for him
That the sender was dim,
And the detonator was bound to fail.

ISSY

There was a lazy man called Issy
Who pretended to keep very busy.
By this sort of quirk
He avoided hard work,
But got everyone else in a tizzy.

IVAN

There was a young singer called Ivan
Who sought his song to enliven.
But his syncopation
Caused consternation,
And they told him to stop his contrivin'.

IVOR

There was a young man called Ivor
Well known as an expert survivor.
No need to guess,
He was ex-SAS
Who could live for a week on a fiver.

IVY

There was a young dancer called Ivy
Whose style was all twisted and jivey.
When asked how to do it,
She said, "There's nothing to it,
I eat worms all wriggly and writhy."

IZAAK. SEE ISAAC.

IZZY

There was a young toper[63] called Izzy
Who didn't like drinks that were fizzy.
Once, by mistake,
He drank tonic with cake
And worked himself into a tizzy.

---

[63] Toper: (archaic) alcoholic.

J

A loquacious young girl called Joan...

JACK

A young cub reporter called Jack
Was just a literary hack.
He could write good prose
When the need arose,
But the editor gave him the sack.

JACKALYN (ALSO JACQUELINE AND JACQUELYN)

A cheerful young girl called Jackalyn
Had a most infectious grin.
It would start with her mouth
And then move south
Until it covered her chin.

JACKI (ALSO JACKIE, JACKY AND JACQUI)

A muddled young girl called Jackie
Had habits extremely tacky.
While decorating her rooms
With cheap heirlooms,
She'd chew on an old quid of baccy.

JACOB

A smart young man called Jacob
Applied to a firm for a job.
They offered him work
With food and a perk
As a valet to a rich nabob.

JACQUELINE. SEE JACKALYN.

JACQUELYN. SEE JACKALYN.

JACQUES

An experienced PC called Jacques
Obviously had just what it takes.
He could spot the bad guys,
Arrest the mad spies,
And capture poisonous snakes.

JACQUI. SEE JACKI.

JADE

A cheeky young girl called Jade
Had a job as a lady's maid.
But her apple-pie bed
Made the lady see red,
So she was sacked and never got paid.

JAKE

A cunning young man called Jake
Is really an audacious fake.
I know he's two-faced
I can tell from the taste
When he claims that this scone's a home-bake.

JAMES

A flirtatious man called James
Was always chasing the dames.
When I said, "That one's mine!"
He counted to nine,
Then started calling me names.

JAMIE

There was a young chef called Jamie
Who said, "I'm sure you can't blame me;
It wasn't my fault
There was no salt
And the meat is ripe and so gamy."

JANE

A strange young girl called Jane
We thought was rather inane.
She'd remove her hat,
Take in the cat,
Then go for a walk in the rain.

JANET

There was an odd being called Janet
Who came from another planet.
Instead of legs
She had wheels on pegs
And her head was mainly of granite.

JANEY

A young Met girl called Janey
Was known to be ever so brainy.
She could forecast the weather
With the aid of a feather,
And could tell it was going to be rainy.

JANICE

An eccentric young girl called Janice
Said to me, "I like dancing and this."
When I enquired of the latter
She started to flatter,
Then told me she'd just like a kiss.

JANIE. SEE JANEY.

JANIS. SEE JANICE.

JASMINE

A lady professor called Jasmine
Was an expert in the study of plasmine.[64]
But she failed to spot
An incipient clot,
And became widely known as a has-been.

JASON

A man in a hurry called Jason
Had a haircut using a basin.
It was very bad luck
When that vessel got stuck
But the fire service said they would hasten.

JASPER

An obstinate boy named Jasper
Always called a file a rasper.
He was often heard
To use the alternative word,
Such as calling a fag a gasper.

JEAN

A lonely young girl called Jean
Was rarely, if ever, seen.
She lived in a flat
With a dog and a cat
And a sort of in-between.

JEANETTE

An impecunious girl called Jeanette
Claimed she was never in debt.
She'd borrow from her brothers
To pay off some others
Then borrow again, but forget.

---

[64] Plasmine: a protein in the plasma of the blood.

JEANNE. SEE JEAN.

JEFF

> A budding composer called Jeff
> Thought that he'd become tone deaf.
> His dominant chord
> Was found to be flawed
> And he'd forgotten to note down the clef.

JEFFREY. SEE GEOFFREY.

JEMIMA

> There was a young linguist called Jemima
> Who learnt Latin from her old school primer.
> The first declension
> Was beyond comprehension,
> And she felt Greek was somewhat sublimer.

JENNIE (ALSO JENNY)

> There was a young peach called Jennie
> Whose suitors were varied and many.
> Then along came a sire –
> Her true heart's desire –
> And she had no more suitors – not any.

JEREMY

> A garrulous young man called Jeremy
> I fear would always weary me.
> He never ceased talking,
> While long-distance walking.
> He said he'd stop when they bury me.

JEROME

There was a young poet called Jerome
Whose pride and joy was his tome.
He'd carry it around
The London Underground,
I wish he'd leave it at home!

JERRARD. SEE GERARD.

JERRY. SEE GERRY.

JESS

A prodigal man called Jess
Was prone to wanton excess.
He'd spend all his wage
Then get in a rage,
So they put him under duress.

JESSICA

Said a naïve penniless girl called Jessica
"I pay too much for my brassica.
The land of the free
Sounds just right for me
So I'm off to live in America."

JESSIE (ALSO JESSY)

A young Scottish girl called Jessie
Once caught a quick glimpse of Nessie.[65]
When asked to describe it,
She said, "I can't abide it,
It was just so monstrous and messy."

---

[65] Nessie: a colloquial name for the Loch Ness Monster.

JILL

A friend of young Jack called Jill
Was the one who climbed up that hill.
She met with defeat
During this epic feat
And marks out of ten were nil.

JILLIAN. SEE GILLIAN.

JILLY. SEE GILLIE.

JIM

There was a landlubber called Jim
Who put out to sea on a whim.
But a whim's not a boat,
And it just would not float,
So his survival prospects were grim.

JIMMIE (ALSO JIMMY)

A scatter-brained man called Jimmie
Was known to be awfully whimmy.
When he found life a bind
He'd make up his mind,
Then dance a sinuous shimmy.

JO (ALSO JOE)

A budding young cook called Jo
Said to me, "Well, wadda yer know?
I baked this bun
At gas mark one,
But I find that was much too low."

JOAN

A loquacious young girl called Joan
Was perpetually using the phone.
She stayed there all day
Just having her say,
Till her ear took the shape of a cone.

JOANNA

There was a stern girl – Joanna,
Who had an authoritarian manner.
She banned all cats
In council flats
When she became the district planner.

JOANNE (ALSO JO ANNE)

There was an old lady – Joanne
Who travelled around by sedan.
I don't mean the litter
With just the one sitter
But a limousine driven by a man.

JOCK

There was a young piper called Jock
Who removed his bagpipes from hock.
But he heard people's moans
When he started the drones
Which gave his ego a knock.

JOE. SEE JO.

JOEY

There was an old vagrant called Joey
Who had no money for food, so 'e
Begged on the street
For something to eat,
With his eyes all humble and doe-y.

Joel

There was a young tenor called Joel
Who had to throw in the towel.
It restricted his scope,
For he hadn't a hope.
When he ruined *The First Noël*.

John (also Jon)

An undergraduate called John
Was encouraged to train as a don.
His call on the Master
Of Kings was disaster,
And he said it was all just a con.

Johnnie (also Johnny)

A silly young man called Johnnie,
Kept singing, "Nonny nay nonnie."
I said, "Please stop
Or I'll just call a cop."
But he didn't think that very fonny.

Jon. See John.

Jonas

There was a nitpicker called Jonas
Who was one of life's great moaners.
But once in a while
He was known to smile –
When they gave him his Christmas bonus.

Jonathon

There was a rich man called Jonathon
Who ran in the London marathon.
His footman ran alongside
Refreshments to provide,
And his valet was ready with the bath on.

JORDAN

A happy but poor man called Jordan
Used to drive a very old Morgan.
As he went along
He would sing a song
Whilst playing a small mouth organ.

JOSEPH

There was a young lisper called Joseph
Who said, "I must water my roseph.
But first I'll dead head
The ones in that bed,
And then pick a bunch of nice posieph."

JOSEPHINE

There was a brave soldier – Josephine,
Well-known as a warrior queen.
She'd make brilliant attacks
With her battle axe,
Then offer her foes codeine.

JOSHUA

A stylish young man called Joshua
Said to his friend, "How posh you are!"
His friend got elated
And then reciprocated:
"You are too, by gosh you are!"

JOSIAH

A fearless young chap called Josiah
Was just the kind of man I admire.
He was noble and brave,
Was nobody's slave,
And the right sort of type to inspire.

JOY

An archaeological student called Joy
Once paid a short visit to Troy.
She started to dig
And danced a jig
When she discovered a Bronze Age toy.

JOYCE

A car enthusiast called Joyce
Went and bought an ancient Rolls Royce.
With a car so classic,
She was quite ecstatic
Until she received the invoice.

JUDIE (ALSO JUDY)

There was a young girl called Judie
Who liked to play hot boogie-woogie.
She could play the base
Until blue in the face,
It was the treble that made her all moody.

JULIA

There was a weird girl called Julia
Who we all thought was most peculiar.
To play us a trick,
She'd pretend to be sick,
Then say she was just out to fool yer.

JULIAN

An ambitious young man called Julian
Set out to make his first million.
He used a detector
Lent by his rector
And found a rich source of bullion.

JULIE

There was a business lady called Julie
Whose staff was just one coolie.
He worked all day
From April to May,
Then was sacked for being unruly.

JULIETTE

A fearless young girl called Juliette
Went and climbed up a crane for a bet.
She was forced to stop
Halfway to the top;
She'll come down one day, but not yet.

JUNE

A silly beach girl called June
Once buried herself in a dune.
When she couldn't get out
She started to shout,
But was stuck there all afternoon.

JUSTIN

There was a young cyclist called Justin
Who found his old bike was rustin'.
He scraped it clean
Till quite pristine.
Then found it needed some dustin'.

JUSTINA

A young Arab girl called Justina
Used to play an old concertina.
She'd darn some socks
While she squeezed the box;
For watching she'd charge you one dinar.

JUSTINE

A wild Scottish girl – Justine,
Was a bit of a libertine.
But they taught her a lesson
In the Court of Session
When they placed her in quarantine.

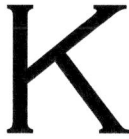

A lugubrious young man called Kerry...

Karen (pronounced Karren)

An aristocratic girl called Karen
Got married to a bold bad baron.
It was anyone's guess
How the new baroness
Booked him so early with Charon.[66]

Karl. See Carl.

Kate

A maddening young girl called Kate
Was always making me wait.
We were to be wed,
But at last I saw red,
And when she arrived – 'twas too late.

Katharine. See Catherine.

Katerina (also Katrina)

A calm young girl – Katerina
Once fell into a big cat arena.
But she kept quite cool
Sat down on a stool,
And played tunes on her ocarina.

Katherine. See Catherine.

Kathleen

There was a young girl – Kathleen,
A bright little Irish colleen.
She was really quite placid
Unless she felt acid,
Then she gave vent to her spleen.

---

[66] Charon: the fabled ferryman of Hades.

KATHI / KATHIE. SEE CATHIE.

KATHRYN. SEE CATHERINE.

KATHY. SEE CATHY.

KATRINA. SEE KATERINA.

KATRIN

A baffling young girl called Katrin
Used to wear a perpetual grin.
She had the smile
Throughout a murder trial,
Putting the jury into a spin.

KAY

A computer operator called Kay
Was always losing her way.
When she was sent to York
She arrived in Cork
So was sacked the very next day.

KEITH

There was a young PC called Keith
Who joined the police in Leith.
But the Super said, "No,
You'll just have to go.
I can't get your name around my teeth."

KELLY

An over-weight woman called Kelly
Used to wobble like the proverbial jelly.
When told she might die,
She just said, "Oh fie!
I won't – no, not on your Nellie."

KEN (ALSO KENN)

A backward young boy called Ken
Was unable to count up to ten.
We thought that fruition
Might result from tuition,
But the only question was, "When?"

KENNETH

An energetic old man called Kenneth
Declared, "I have passed my zenith.
I've developed a lisp.
And my words aren't crisp,
But is there anyone here for tennith?"

KENNIE (ALSO KENNY)

There was an old shopkeeper called Kennie,
Who sold sweets for just two a penny.
They told him, "That's dear.
And we think it unfair.
It's really a ha'penny too many."

KERRY

A lugubrious young man called Kerry
Once drank a whole bottle of sherry.
The sad look on his face
Disappeared without trace
As he then commenced to make merry.

KEVIN

A boastful young man called Kevin
Claimed his father knew Ernest Bevin.
I told him, "So what!
I don't care a jot
My father used to play for André Previn."

KIERAN

A valiant young man called Kieran
Was bold and dashing and darin'.
But when his wife said a spider
Was sitting beside her
He suddenly lost all his hearin'.

KIM

An agile young man called Kim
Was exceedingly good at gym.
He'd walk on his hands
To amuse his fans
While singing a Christmas hymn.

KIM

There's a nubile young girl called Kim
Whose figure is lovely and slim.
You could never find
One quite so kind,
So why on earth is she marrying *him*?

KIRSTEEN

An eager young girl – Kirsteen,
Just wanted to enjoy Halloween.
But she thought it absurd
To cut out a gourd,
And wear it so she couldn't be seen.

KIRSTIE (ALSO KIRSTY)

There was a young golfer called Kirstie
Who sliced her drive on the first tee.
She then took a stroll
To the nineteenth hole
Saying she was ever so thirsty.

KIT

A young maidservant called Kit
Tried to carry out a midnight flit.
By the break of day
She had lost her way,
And said she felt a bit of a twit.

KITTI (ALSO KITTY)

A beautiful young girl called Kitti
Wanted to leave the great big city.
She wished to reside
In the countryside
Which her suitors thought was a pity.

KONRAD. SEE CONRAD.

KURT

An unpleasant young man called Kurt
Used to be off-handed and pert.
When he changed his name
He wasn't the same
For now he's an outrageous flirt.

KYLIE

There was a young girl we called Kylie
Of whom people thought very highly.
I asked the explanation
For such veneration.
"It's because I'm tall," she said dryly.

L

A so-called comic called Lester...

LACHLAN

There was a young Scot called Lachlan
Who lived in a hillside clachan.[67]
He was sombre and sad,
And made sporrans and plaid
And kilts from pieces of bracken.

LACHIE (ALSO LACHY)

There was another young Scot called Lachie
Who everyone said was quite whacky.
With considerable pride
He would swim the Clyde,
Whilst smoking his favourite baccy.

LAETITIA (ALSO LETITIA)

A quiet young teenager called Laetitia
Once joined the local militia.
When she tried to stifle
The noise from her rifle,
The CO threatened to ditch her.

LANA

An exotic pet lover called Lana
Once tried to tame an iguana.
It would stand on one leg
Or sit up and beg
When she gave it a piece of banana.

LANCE

A foxtrot expert called Lance
Always took giant strides at a dance.
He once took the floor
Went right through the door,
And found himself half way to France.

---

[67] Clachan: (Scottish) a small village.

LANCELOT

An energetic young man called Lancelot
Was always able to dance a lot.
He had a good samba
But a terrible mamba,
And I'm afraid he tended to prance a lot.

LARA

There was a young countess called Lara
Who lived on the edge of the Sahara.
For an all-over tan
She'd wear just a fan
And sometimes her best tiara.

LARAINE

There was a dozy girl called Laraine
Who told me I was going insane.
When I asked her why,
She didn't reply,
Then said she couldn't explain.

LARRY

Said a young bachelor called Larry,
"I'm afraid I'll never ever marry.
But it's quite okay,
I like it this way,
I'm not just a Tom, Dick or Harry."

LAUNCELOT

My wife knows a ghost called Launcelot
Whose trouble is that he haunts a lot.
But this busy spectre
Does not affect her,
In fact she says he daunts her not.

LAURA

A lover of nature was poor Laura
Who liked to study fauna and flora.
She thought she was concealed
That day in a field,
Hoping the bull would ignore her.

LAUREN

A kilted young girl called Lauren
Always wore an extra-large sporran.
Some said the fur
Was likely to purr,
And the Tom it came from was foreign.

LAURETTA

A frightened young girl called Lauretta
Said someone was out to get her.
She was in a bad mood
Because of a feud
And had an unwilling part in a vendetta.

LAURENCE (ALSO LAWRENCE)

A sensitive young man called Laurence
Viewed all onions with abhorrence.
He said, "I'm allergic
To things so acerbic,
And my tears just come down in torrents."

LAURIE (ALSO LAWRIE)

There was a man-hunter called Laurie
Who all day had stalked his quarry.
He started to swear
When he finally got near,
For his target escaped in a lorry.

Laurie (also Lawrie)

There was an apprentice named Laurie
Who worked in the firm called MORI.[68]
She was a minion
Without an opinion.
She was rude and never said "Sorry".

Lavinia

A young oceanographer called Lavinia
Just wanted to study actinia.[69]
She had to strive
To keep some alive
But all of them just got skinnier.

Lawrence. See Laurence.

Lawrie. See Laurie.

Lazarus

There was an old barber called Lazarus
Who made our lives somewhat hazardous.
It wasn't the trim
That was so grim –
His chatter was so cantankerous.

Lear (also Leah)

A fashionable girl called Lear
Said she didn't know what to wear.
But all my life
I've heard my wife
Make similar remarks I fear.

---

[68] MORI: Marketing and Opinion Research Institute.

[69] Actinia: the sea-anemone.

LEE (ALSO LEIGH)

A foolish young sailor called Lee
Was found adrift out at sea.
The rescuers said,
"You would soon have been dead,
So we insist on charging a fee."

LEILA (PRONOUNCED LIE-LA)

There was a young athlete called Leila
Who was known as a very fast miler.
She won an award
For a world record
When she outpaced an angry Rottweiler.

LEMMIE

There was a young actor called Lemmie
Who lived in a rather cramped semi.
But he made his name
And gained considerable fame
When he won a coveted Emmy.

LEN

There was an old farmer called Len
Who said that he lived by his pen.
But he had me fooled
For my leg he had pulled,
And I learnt that his sheep numbered ten.

LENA

In Rome, a young slave called Lena
Once faced an angry hyena.
Quick as a flash
She gave it a bash,
And knocked it from the arena.

LENNIE (ALSO LENNY)

An enterprising man called Lennie
Once found an old spinning jenny.
He made some thread,
Which he coloured deep red
And sold for two reels a penny.

LEO

There was a young man called Leo
Who formed a musical trio.
It went down a treat
In places like Crete,
But was booed off the stage in Rio.

LEON

There was a young man called Leon
Who I thought was having me on.
He said, "I'm going away
For a year and a day,
And will become a Chilean peon."

LEONARD

There was a keen soldier, Leonard,
Who worked his men so hard.
They would run for miles
Carrying quarry tiles,
Then do extra duty on guard.

LEONORA

There was an old seer called Leonora
Who exuded a mysterious aura.
It was said she foretold
The end of the world,
But I thought it best to ignore 'er.

LEOPOLD

A pioneering young man – Leopold
Went off to search for some gold.
He panned in a stream
All day, it would seem.
Then went off home with a cold.

LESLIE

Said a businessman called Leslie,
"I'm afraid you just depress me.
I know your cash flow
Will reach a new low,
But you'll just have to charge much less fee."

LESTER

A so-called comic called Lester
Was taken on as the new court jester.
But the king soon said:
"Go, take off his head!
This oaf is starting to pester."

LETITIA. SEE LAETITIA.

LETTICE

In Nepal a young girl called Lettice
Came across a small group of yetis.
When they saw her they sang
In accented Tamang;[70]
"Could you please just tell us where Tibet is?"

---

[70] Tamang: one of the languages of Nepal.

Lettie (also Letty)

There was a silly girl called Lettie
Who carelessly stepped off the jetty.
To cover her confusion
She had excuses in profusion
And said that I pushed her – how petty!

Liam

A short-sighted man called Liam,
Said to me, "You really must see 'em.
Those people, I mean,
They're all painted green.
And I'd rather see 'em than be 'em."

Libby

There was a young child called Libby
Who would dribble right down her bibby.
At times she would mutter
And gurgle and splutter;
I think she was trying to rib me.

Lil

An eccentric old lady called Lil
Always left me to pay the bill.
I just hope it was true
When she said, "I thank you,
I'll remember you in my will."

LILITH (ALSO LYNETTE)

An archaeological student called Lilith
Sat the whole day on a trilith.[71]
Despite the pain
She did it again.
Now, what do you think she is ill with?

LILLIAN

A nubile young girl called Lillian
Once met a swarthy old Chilean.
He said, "Marry me!"
She replied, "Fiddle-de-dee,
I would if you had fifty million."

LILY

An eccentric young girl called Lily
Was thought by all to be silly.
If we forgave her a sin
She'd just give a grin.
Then do it again willy nilly.

LINDA (ALSO LYNDA)

There was a girl guide called Linda
Who lit a campfire with some tinder.
The fire got too hot
For things in the pot,
And her spuds were all burnt to a cinder.

---

[71] Trilith: a prehistoric monument consisting of two upright stones with a third resting between them.

Linette

A rather fast girl called Linette
Started life as a brunette.
She changed it to blue,
Then used H_2O_2,[72]
Which was something she grew to regret.

Linsay (also Lindsay)

There was a rich man called Linsay,
Who said, "Any girl who wins me
Can have half my estate
And share my fate,
But she must know a cure for quinsy."[73]

Lionel

A foolish young man called Lionel
Once took a small sip of trional.[74]
He awoke from a trance
In the centre of France
Wearing nothing but pants made of vinyl.

Lisa

There was a young tourist called Lisa
Who visited the tower of Pisa.
She called for the arrest
Of an Italian pest
Who said he wanted to "kees 'er!"

Lisbeth. See Elizabeth.

Lizbeth. See Elizabeth.

---

[72] H_2O_2: Hydrogen Peroxide, a bleaching agent.

[73] Quinsy: an inflammation of the throat, especially the tonsils.

[74] Trional: a hypnotic drug.

LIZ

A silly young girl called Liz
Took part in a popular quiz.
But she earned no fee
When she told the MC
To go and mind his own biz.

LIZA

I didn't know that a girl called Liza
Had always been an early riser.
So my joke fell flat,
When I wore a funny hat,
And called at six to surprise her.

LIZZIE (ALSO LIZZY)

A pretty young girl called Lizzie
Used to put all the boys in a tizzy.
When they made a date
And then arrived late
She'd say, "Go away, I'm too busy."

LLEWELYN

There was a strong man called Llewelyn
Whose hobby was just tree fellin'.
His present habitat
Didn't suit that,
No, not the Garden City of Welwyn.

LLOYD (ALSO LOYD)

There was a young toper called Lloyd
Who said there were things he enjoyed.
As a pioneer
He liked his beer,
But rum was a drink to avoid.

LOLITA

I knew an aging girl called Lolita
Who was always adjusting my heater.
She said she was cold;
I said, "Well, you're old.
I'm not and I pay by the litre."

LOLLY

At Christmas, a girl called Lolly
Once stole a small piece of holly.
But a night in jail
With no chance of bail
Made her reassess her folly.

LOREN

There was a strange girl called Loren
Who denied that she was foreign.
But she had no idea
Of the price of a beer,
And had never heard of a florin.

LORENZO

A young bell ringer called Lorenzo
Could never say what he meant, so
He told me in mime
That the faulty chime
Was due to the clapper being bent so.

LORETTA

There was a new soprano called Loretta
Who had a part in an operetta.
The star was enraged
When he was upstaged,
But it didn't seem to upset her.

LORNA

I once knew a girl called Lorna.
I wish now I'd thought to warn her
That the lock on the door
Wouldn't work any more,
So she was boiled to death in the sauna.

LORRAINE

There was a young sailor – Lorraine,
Who sailed the Spanish Main.
When she reached Tortuga
She pawned her old Luger,
Then sailed right back again.

LOTTIE

A society girl we called Lottie
Always said that her problem was knotty.
Her hairs would split,
And her dress wouldn't fit…
She really drove me quite potty.

LOU

A Venus-like girl called Lou
Had eyes of the deepest blue,
For a very small fee,
She would gaze out to sea,
And ships altered course for the view.

LOUIS

There was a young Texan called Louis
Who said, "Do tell me what a *queue* is."
I said, "You call it a *line*,
Which I think is fine,
But it depends what your point of view is."

LOUISE

There was a young driver called Louise
Whose nose was inclined to freeze.
The sight of her conk
Made motorists honk,
But the noise would be drowned by her sneeze.

LOWELL

There was a young graduate called Lowell
Whom most people said was a know-all.
I know they were wrong
When he said King Kong
Once tried to sing *The First Noël*.

LOYD. SEE LLOYD.

LUCE

There was a young flirt called Luce
Who used to play fast and loose.
That is until,
On a sacred hill,
She met that god known as Zeus.

LUCIAN

There was a young tutor called Lucian
Who became a good Confucian.
He extolled many things,
And walked with kings,
Whilst teaching them elocution.

LUCIUS

A strange Eastern man called Lucius
Informed us he'd met Confucius.
We said this was wrong,
He was still in Hong Kong.
And he'd never paid what was due to us.

LUCILLE

There was a young roofer – Lucille,
Who said, "You're as young as you feel."
After a night on the tiles
She'd run ten miles,
Then dance to her glockenspiel.[75]

LUCINDA

A careless a young girl called Lucinda
Set fire to a small box of tinder.
No, don't be a mystic,
Or become sadistic,
She was never burnt to a cinder.

LUCRETIA

A balding young girl called Lucretia
Suffered from severe alopecia.[76]
The best hair restorer
Was species of flora,
Mixed up with milk of magnesia.

LUCRETIUS

An irritating youth called Lucretius
Was inclined to be somewhat facetious.
When really small
He was rude to us all,
But most of all to his teachers.

---

[75] Glockenspiel: a musical instrument consisting of series of bells or metal bars or tubes suspended or mounted in a frame and struck by hammers.

[76] Alopecia: the absence of hair from areas of the body where it normally grows; baldness.

LUCY

A brainy young girl called Lucy
Was determined to become a QC.
She came out best
In every stiff test,
And the briefs they gave her were juicy.

LUDOVIC (ALSO LUDOVICK)

There was an odd man called Ludovic
Who was thought to be rude and thick.
He would swing the lead
By retiring to bed,
And everyone said he was "pseudo-sick".

LUKE

I first met a man called Luke
When he worked in an Arabian souk.
His name's now in lights,
He's reached dizzy heights,
And I find they've made him a duke.

LULU

I once said to a girl called Lulu,
"It's many years ago that I knew you.
Your words at the time
Were mostly in mime
And all you could say was 'goo goo'."

LUTHER

A peerless young man called Luther
Was known to nearly always do the
Paramount thing.
He was the king;
I've never known anyone smoother.

LYDIA

An astute young girl known as Lydia
At auctions would always out bid yer.
She'd buy odds and ends
Such as lamps and old pens.
And when she resold – then she did yer.

LYN (ALSO LYNN)

There was a strange man called Lyn
Who made his home in a bin.
He said it would please
Men like Diogenes,[77]
An explanation I thought a bit thin.

LYNDA. SEE LINDA.

LYNETTE. SEE LINETTE.

---

[77] Diogenes: Greek philosopher 445–c.365 BC, who was alleged to have lived in a tub.

M

There was a young builder called Micky…

MAB

A podgy young angler called Mab
Wanted to get rid of some flab.
Her weight kept on growing
So she thought she'd try rowing,
And managed to catch a crab.[78]

MABEL

A fashionable young girl called Mabel
Once wore a coat made of sable.
That's what she thought,
But she really got caught,
It said "imitation" on the label.

MABS

A young street trader called Mabs
Said she'd try selling kebabs.
But it was all such a waste
For they lacked any taste
Till she added some sauce made in labs.

MADDY

A girl with strange tastes was Maddy
For she ate nothing but finnan haddie.[79]
She'd scoff it all day
If someone would pay.
Then she found him – a nice sugar daddy.

---

[78] 'Catch a crab': in rowing, to sink the oars too much or too little.

[79] Finnan haddie: (Scottish) finnan haddock.

MADGE

There was a young schoolgirl called Madge
Who was given a buttonhole badge.
It was from her class
Who voted this lass
The one most likely to cadge.

MADONNA

A noble young girl called Madonna
Used to quote, "Death before dishonour!"
And her words were truly meant
As a statement of intent,
For now I fear she's a goner.

MAE

There was a simple young girl called Mae
Who had practically nothing to say.
Which was just as well
For it was hard to tell
Whether what she said was okay.

MAEVE

There was a gauche girl called Maeve
Who tried very hard to save.
At the end of a year
She bought a large beer.
And spent the rest on a rave.

MAG

A strangely dressed girl called Mag
Used to say, "I don't like to brag,
But I'm a millionaire
With never a care,
Although I might look like a hag."

MAGDALENE

An excited young girl, Magdalene,
Went to town every Halloween.
But a country bumpkin
Just quashed her new pumpkin;
After that she wasn't so keen.

MAGGIE

There was an old woman called Maggie
Whose face was scrawny and craggy.
She liked nothing better
Than to walk her red setter
And tell tales that were obviously shaggy.

MAGNUS

There was a young singer called Magnus
Who wanted to sing "Dei Agnus".
When we said to him "No,
We'd prefer you to go."
He said he'd just keep on naggin' us.

MAISIE

A beautiful young girl called Maisie
Once told me that I was just crazy.
I said, "Yes, my dear,
About *you*, d'ye hear?"
The rest of the evening was hazy.

MALACHI

There was a young man – Malachi,
Who wouldn't eat blackberry pie.
Instead he'd eat toffee
Washed down with coffee,
Saying, "What a nice way to die!"

MALLY

A very fast driver called Mally
Took part in a motor car rally.
He had a girl on his lap
To read the map,
But she went badly astray in a valley.

MAMIE

A young shop assistant called Mamie
Said, "You really can't blame me;
I cannot work well
When there's nothing to sell –
And anyway, why don't you pay me?"

MANDY

There was a young toper called Mandy
Who drank half a bottle of brandy.
As she staggered up stairs
She saw two pink bears
Drinking a ginger beer shandy.

MANUEL

There was a young peon called Manuel
Who was locked in a Chilean cell.
But he avoided his plight
By escaping that night.
Without stopping to say farewell.

MARCEL

There was a young thief called Marcel
Whose fate was due to tar smell.
He didn't know he smelt
When he stole the asphalt.
Now he's in a solitary far cell.

MARCUS

There was a spiteful man called Marcus
Who went out of his way to nark us.
Sometimes I feel
We should make a deal,
Or I swear I'll dance on his carcass.

MARGARET

There was a new driver called Margaret
Whose car got stuck in a rut.
Two sly-looking men
Said, "We'll free you and then
We insist on having our cut."

MARGERY (ALSO MARJORY, MARJORIE)

A geneticist and apiarist[80] – Margery,
Claimed she could make a larger bee.
With a growth hormone
She made a large drone,
Which was promptly banned by decree.

MARGO

There was a young poet called Margo
Who hid herself in some cargo.
To pass the time
She produced a rhyme
As a refrain for Handel's Largo.

MARGUERITA

A river-bathing girl – Marguerita,
Saw a croc that she thought might eat her.
As she swam for the shore
On the bank she saw
A lioness just waiting to greet her.

---

[80] Apiarist: person who cares for bees; bee-keeper.

MARGUERITE

There was a young girl – Marguerite,
Who possessed such odd-shaped feet.
The outline of her heel
Looked quite unreal,
But at least it was small and neat.

MARIAN

A misogamist[81] of a girl called Marian
Told me, "I ain't a goin' a marryin',
I do not like men –
Except now and then –
When they do my fetchin' and carryin'."

MARIANNE

A nymph of a girl called Marianne
Declared that she had developed a plan.
"I'm going to start a lottery
In that old pottery
And the prize I give will be – a man!"

MARIETTA

A rather wet girl called Marietta
Said she should have known better.
She went there and back
Without her old mac
In order to post her dad's letter.

MARIGOLD

There was a young child – Marigold,
Who found out that she'd been sold.
But it would seem
She was the cream,
And her price was increased fourfold.

---

[81] Misogamist: someone who hates marriage.

MARILYN

A voracious young girl called Marilyn
Would overeat but remain quite thin.
She had a large dinner
But got even thinner;
It seems that she just couldn't win.

MARINA

A beanpole of a girl called Marina
Used to get leaner and leaner.
That might be okay,
But I just have to say
That she also got meaner and meaner.

MARIO

There was a young dramatist – Mario,
Who wrote a broad scenario.
He outlined each role,
With a long rigmarole
But kept the part of Lothario.

MARJORIE. SEE MARGERY.

MARJORY. SEE MARGERY.

MARION

A would-be musician called Marion
Once aspired to play the clarion.
I'm afraid her style
Made us run a mile,
And it frightened the crows from the carrion.

MARK

There was a young scientist called Mark
Who said he'd bottled a quark.
If they confirmed his claim
He'd have enduring fame,
But he admitted it was all just a lark.

MARMADUKE

There's an annoying young man – Marmaduke,
Whom I'm never able to rebuke.
He has the last say
In just every way.
I put it all down to a fluke.

MARTA

A hard-bitten old girl called Marta
Was known as a bit of a tartar.
She was very tough
Lived quite rough,
And did her business by barter.

MARTHA

A precocious young child called Martha
Would not let anyone bath her.
I know that she got
A good smack on her bot,
And was told to shower if she'd rather.

MARTI (ALSO MARTY)

A boisterous young girl called Marti
Was full of fun, and so hearty.
When she took to the floor,
We all knew the score:
She'd be the life and soul of the party.

MARTIN (ALSO MARTYN)

There's a strange old man called Martin
Whose legs, one might say, are thin.
There's one narrow bone
On its very own,
And something that looks like a pin.

MARTY. SEE MARTI.

MARTYN. SEE MARTIN.

MARVIN

There was a new chef called Marvin
Who said he'd do the carvin'.
When he took so long
Some played ping-pong,
While others just sat there starvin'.

MARY

There was a tough girl called Mary
Who liked manly chests that were hairy.
She had one pal
Who was Neanderthal.
Mary was too, that's my theory.

MARY ANN

There was a young girl, Mary Ann,
Who kept wine in an old jerrican.
She said, "Water's oppressive,
This might be excessive;
But come, let's make merry, man."

MARYELE

There was a young wife called Maryele
Who brought up her family very well.
One child could walk
Another could talk,
And the third could do a merry yell.

MAT (ALSO MATT)

There was a young man called Mat
Who captured a vampire bat.
It never drank blood
It just chewed the cud
Then went to sleep on his hat.

MATHIAS

There was a young curate called Mathias
Who was known to be extremely pious.
He wore his knees flat
And not only that,
He sought more disciples – but why us?

MATILDA

There once was a spy called Matilda
Who was captured by the foe, who grilled her.
Her cover was real
So they gave her a meal.
But she was ever so narked when they billed her.

MATT. SEE MAT.

MATTHEW

There was an old man called Matthew
Who was told his wig was askew.
When he'd put it right
He said, "What a sight,
That's something I have to renew."

MAUDLIN

An ambitious young girl called Maudlin
Was often accused of dawdlin'.
She said, "I might amble
When I'm on a ramble,
But watch me when I'm after a lordlin'!"

MAUREEN

A young Irish girl called Maureen
Used to ride down a leafy boreen.[82]
She rode bareback
On a steady old hack
To get to the local shebeen.[83]

MAURICE (ALSO MORRIS)

A transport employer called Maurice
Had trouble with some of his lorries.
A clutch was slipping,
A tipper wasn't tipping,
And he was due in an hour at the quarries.

MAVIS

A muddy young girl called Mavis
Asked her mum if she knew what a knave is.
Her mum said, "My dear,
It'll soon become clear,
Meanwhile I'll show what to lave is."[84]

---

[82] Boreen: (Irish) a bridle path or lane.

[83] Shebeen: (Irish & Scottish) an unlicensed house selling alcoholic liquor.

[84] Lave: wash, bathe.

MAX

An old hypochondriac called Max
Was forever visiting quacks.
He would always endure
Every pill or a cure,
But on getting the bill he'd make tracks.

MAXIMILIAN

A brash young man – Maximilian,
Found his father had left him a million.
He shouted, "Hurray!
I'll spend it today."
And painted the town bright vermilion.

MAY

There was a young girl called May
Who declared she'd always obey.
She omitted to mention
It was her intention
To always have the last say.

MEG

A one-legged girl called Meg
Used to drink strong beer from a keg.
She'd then stagger home
With an old metronome
Ticking in time with her leg.

MEGAN

A sharp shooting girl called Megan
Invented a new type of egg gun.
In a target test
It was almost the best
But finished up just level peggin'.

MEL

A tease of a girl called Mel
Once said that she just wouldn't tell.
There were but a few
Who knew what she knew,
And the rest of us suffered like hell.

MELANIE

A young wayward girl called Melanie
Told me she'd committed a felony.
When I asked, "What sort?"
All she did was retort,
"Take your pick of the miscellany."

MELISSA

There was a pretty girl called Melissa
Who said I was the first to kiss her.
She was just a young lass
At the time, but alas,
Her dad saw me – how I miss her!

MELODY

There was a Scots girl – Melody,
Who said, "Och, what a dull yellow dee!
With fog sae thick
It's made me sick,
Ah'm gang' off home for ma tea."

MEREDITH

I heard tell of an Irishman called Meredith
Who was not the sort of man to be merry with.
He was just the sort of bloke
Who couldn't see a joke
And was known to us as the Kerry myth.

MERIEL

A horrid old woman called Meriel
Would breakfast on three types of cereal.
She choked on some toast.
Then gave up the ghost;
And nobody came to her burial.

MERYL

There was a young girl called Meryl
Whose outlook was distinctly feral.
She tended to evade
The normal trade,
Her ambitions were much more spheral.

MIA

There was a pretty girl called Mia
And everyone wanted to see her.
But her behaviour was crass,
For she brayed like an ass,
And she really was a bit queer.

MICAH

There was a young rambler called Micah
Who toured the world as a hiker.
To accompany his walks
He had two large hawks,
An enormous Great Dane and a duiker.[85]

MICH (ALSO MITCH)

An ambitious young man called Mich
Declared one day he'd be rich.
I can hear you sigh:
"That's just pie in the sky."
But he achieved his aim with no hitch.

---

[85] Duiker: African antelope, usually having a crest of long hair between its horns.

MICHAEL

There was an intellectual named Michael
Whose knowledge was astronomical.
He understood tides
And lots more besides,
And could predict a star's daily cycle.

MICHAELA (WHEN PRONOUNCED MICK-EYE-LA)

A new office member called Michaela
Had a job as an office filer.
But her terrible documentation
Caused chaos and consternation,
So they slipped her a feral Rottweiler.

MICHELLE

There was a young dealer – Michelle,
Who had many odd things to sell.
With the stuffed Tibetan yak,
And some bric-à-brac,
She had potpourri to stifle the smell.

MICK

A man with a limp called Mick
Had a knee that often went click.
He said it was due
To an angry old gnu[86]
Which had caught him once with a kick.

---

[86] Gnu: an antelope native to South Africa.

MICKY

There was a young builder called Micky
Who obtained a job as a bricky.[87]
He was not very fond
Of Flemish Bond
And was sacked when the job got too tricky.

MIKE

A factory worker called Mike
Was always going on strike.
His boss shut the gates
On him and his mates,
And told him to get on his bike.

MILDRED

A young Devon farmer – Mildred,
Was never, ever, ill-fed.
And there was a bounty
In farming that county,
For her fields were always tilled red.[88]

MILES (ALSO MYLES)

A young zoologist called Miles
Used to keep a lot of reptiles.
I found he wasn't there
When I called last year,
But the crocs were wreathed in smiles.

---

[87] Bricky: slang for a bricklayer.

[88] Tilled red: Devon has red soil.

MILLICENT

There was a young deb called Millicent
Who bought from a man some silly scent.
She was put in a coma
By the strange aroma
But was quite knocked out by the bill 'e sent.

MILLIE (ALSO MILLY)

A young partygoer called Millie
Said she felt frightfully silly.
The event took place yearly,
But she came a day early
To the fancy-dress ball as a lily.

MIMI

There was an old girl called Mimi
Whose outlook was always so seamy.
She'd shout to the men
Again and again,
"Why don't you come up and see me?"

MINELLA

A budding young actress called Minella
Used to think she could play Cinderella.
When a crack in her slipper
Just started to nip her,
She tripped and fell down the cellar.

MINNA

A new young cook called Minna
Invited some men to dinner.
When they found the meat tough,
And cried out, "Enough!"
She explained she was just a beginner.

MINNIE

There was a young teenager called Minnie
Whom everyone knew to be skinny.
But she hid the fact
By the simple act
Of stuffing cotton wool up her pinny.

MIRANDA

A forthright young girl called Miranda
Always spoke with very great candour.
But I fear she told lies,
Which upset all the guys,
And raised the height of their dander.

MIRIAM

An excited young babe called Miriam
Once found a tube of Collyrium.[89]
She thought it a breeze
To give it a squeeze
And the result gave her euphoric delirium.

MITCH. SEE MICH.

MOHAMMED

There was a young man called Mohammed,
Who cried, "At last I'm going to be wed!
I have not seen her face
Or felt her embrace,
But she comes from south of the Med."

---

[89] Collyrium: an eye lotion.

MOIRA (ALSO MOYRA)

There was a young gardener called Moira
Who grew a gigantic hoya.[90]
But its apparent domination
Was an abomination,
And gave the poor girl paranoia.

MOLL

There was a Finnish girl called Moll
Who claimed to have sighted a troll.
But they said it was an offence
To erect a large fence
Around a myth – then charge a toll.

MOLLY

An eccentric old lady called Molly
Rode around in a superman trolly.
She used to cry, "Mush!"
And her chauffeur would push.
When it rained she'd put up her brolly.

MONA

A ruthless young girl called Mona
Once asked me if I would clone her.
I said as a favour
For the gift that I gave her
They must both become a blood donor.

MONICA

There was a weird girl called Monica,
Who played a noisy harmonica.
She would sit in a tree
Playing slightly off key,
While chewing a piece of japonica.

---

[90] Hoya: a climbing shrub with pink, white , or yellow waxy flowers.

MONTAGU (ALSO MONTAGUE)

> An exasperating man called Montagu
> Will never do what we want to do.
> He will never say, "Yes."
> He will always digress,
> So I will now transfer him to you.

MORGAN

> There was a strange girl we called Morgan
> Whom some said looked like a Gorgon.
> She had snakes in her hair –
> But who put them there?
> I did while she played the organ.

MORNA

> There was a biologist called Morna
> Who hunted rare flora and fauna.
> Having searched the entire planet
> For a new type of gannet,
> She found one just round the corner.

MORRIS. SEE MAURICE.

MORTIMER

> A fat young man called Mortimer
> Had a friend who went and bought him a
> Tin of thin soup
> And grapefruit to boot,
> And said that would make him "more trimmer".

MORWENNA

> There was a rich girl called Morwenna
> Who was taught by an aged duenna.
> But she could get away
> At the end of the day
> If she slipped the old girl a tenner.

MOSES

There was a young gardener called Moses
Who found something had killed his roses.
I said, "'Twas my cats,
They went a bit bats
When the scent went right up their noses."

MOYRA. SEE MOIRA.

MUNGO

There was a young father called Mungo
Who said, "Where did that last bun go?"
His son wouldn't say
So his pa said, "Okay,
Now tell me just where did your tongue go?"

MURIEL

There was a young Wren called Muriel
Who was really quite mercurial.
She had a new beau
For ever in tow,
Plus a sailor in HMS *Ithurial*.

MURRAY

There was a pet lover called Murray
Who liked animals small and quite furry.
He had no time to find words
To describe birds;
They always seemed to be in a hurry.

MYFANWY

There was a brash girl called Myfanwy
Who said, "We'll go a-courting, can we?"
I said, "But your pa,
Agreed with your ma
To show me the door and then ban me."

MYLES. SEE MILES.

MYRA

There was keen girl called Myra –
And you really had to admire her –
She'd do any job
To earn a few bob.
What a pity I had to fire her.

MYRNA

There was a poor woman called Myrna
Who lived in the city of Smyrna.
When a penniless rake
Kidnapped her by mistake,
He hastily tried to return her.

MYRTLE

A girl in a hurry was Myrtle
She liked to drive fast and to hurtle.
For R and R,[91]
She'd leave her car
And ride on the back of a turtle.

---

[91] R and R: Rest and Recreation.

N

There was a young dancer called Nina...

NADIA

Said a young accountant called Nadia
"There are rules to which I adhere.
So I must refrain
From being profane,
But I can say you had a terrible year."

NADINE

A sweet little girl called Nadine
Once befriended a lonely sardine.
When she told him his mates
Had been put on to plates
His gills went a dark shade of green.

NAILS

There's no such name as Nails
Which quite deflates my sails.
It's Jane once again,
I am going insane.
Now she's gone right off the rails.

For an explanation, see **Brain***.*

NANCY

A Portuguese girl called Nancy
Used to take all the young lads' fancy.
For just one escudo
She would let them try judo;
But anything else was too chancy.

NANNYH

There was a punkah waller called Nannyh
Whose job was to always fan yer.
The job was a man's,
But she owned the fans,
And if you wanted to try, she'd ban yer.

NAOMI

A polite young girl called Naomi
Once met a rude man from Dahomey.[92]
Although much reviled,
Her response was mild:
"I just don't care what you say o' me."

NAPOLEON

There was a young man called Napoleon
Whose methods were cruel and draconian.
You could see from his face
That he lacked good grace,
For he looked like an outer Mongolian.

NARCISSUS

There was a young tailor – Narcissus,
Who was very cross with his missus.
He was cutting some gear
For an earl to wear,
When she'd lost his best pair of scissors.

NAT

A podgy young man called Nat
Said he thought he was getting so fat.
To make a reduction
He tried liposuction.
Then found his chest was too flat.

NATALIA

A beautiful girl called Natalia
Once made a trip to Australia.
And on Bondi beach,
They said, "What a peach!
She has such lovely paraphernalia."

---

[92] Dahomey: the former name of Benin.

NATALIE

A young collector called Natalie
Said she'd read *Lady Chatterley*.
The garden tips were minimal
And mostly subliminal,
And nothing to do with philately.[93]

NATASHA

A long-suffering girl called Natasha
Got married to a Turkish Pasha.
He said that his wife
Had changed his life,
But he still had the right to thrash her.

NATHAN

An anthropologist called Nathan
Once said, "We're the lords of creation!"
When they asked him, "How so?"
He said, "Don't you know?
It's technological information."

NATHANIEL

There was a young gardener – Nathaniel,
Who grew an enormous biannual.
When they asked him how,
He said, "I just plough,
And then I follow the manual."

NEAL (ALSO NEIL)

A dynamic young man called Neal
Was full of verve and zeal.
He said he kept fit
By willpower and grit,
And the fact his nerves were of steel.

---

[93] Philately: the collection and study of postage stamps.

NED

A most refined gentleman called Ned
Confirmed that he'd like to wed.
He declared that he knew
Any girl would do,
But she must be very well bred.

NEDDIE (ALSO NEDDY)

An ambitious young man called Neddie
Told me that life was so heady.
It was quite a shame
When his big moment came.
And he found he was not quite ready.

NEIL. SEE NEAL.

NEL (ALSO NELL)

There was a noisy young girl called Nel
Who went around ringing a bell.
We said, "Stop that row,
You're a silly old cow!"
She obliged, and then she raised hell.

NELLIE (ALSO NELLY)

She walked so strangely did Nellie
For she hopped around on one wellie.
We said, "Where's the other?"
She replied, "Under cover.
I removed it 'cos it's so smelly."

NERISSA

A worried young girl called Nerissa
Asked her new boyfriend to kiss her.
He was going away,
But just wouldn't say
Whether or not he'd miss 'er.

NERYS

There was a young girl called Nerys
Who rode the wheel called a Ferris.
She thought there was a hitch
When she started to itch,
So she dusted herself down with Derris.

NESSA

There was a high flier called Nessa
Who just couldn't stand the pressure.
She tried hard to forget
All about the jet set.
And set up shop in Odessa.

NESSIE (ALSO NESSY)

There was an old bag called Nessie
Whose style was exceedingly dressy.
"Like mutton dressed as lamb,"
To quote an epigram,
And at the table her manners were messy.

NESTA

A sporting young girl called Nesta
Just once took a ride down the Cresta.
She didn't comprehend
She should turn at a bend,
So now has an eternal siesta.

NETTA

There was a desperate girl called Netta
Who married a chronic old debtor.
When the heavy men came
It was always the same:
"We sent the money by letter."

NGAIO

Said a young space girl called Ngaio
"I come from the satellite Io.
I thought my destination
Was to be a space station
But, by Jupiter, this is Ohio!"

NICHOL (ALSO NICOL)

There was a foolish man called Nichol
Who really got out of control.
He once called a royal
A son of the soil,
And didn't observe protocol.

NICHOLA (ALSO NICOLA)

A slightly mad girl called Nichola
Would always fly a foreign tricolour.
She said the juxtaposition
Of the colours in her vision
Was a thing that would always tickle her.

NICHOLAS (ALSO NICOLAS)

We had an old friend called Nicholas
Who went out of his way to tickle us.
When I gave a wriggle,
He started to giggle,
Which made us look quite ridiculous.

NICK

There was a keen actor called Nick
Who applied to work at the Vic.
They turned him down
With a very small frown,
Saying, "No good, you're really too thick."

NICKKI (ALSO NIKKY)

There was a young person called Nickki
Who was always taking the mickey.
When it was done to me,
I counted up to three;
Then things got a little bit tricky.

NICOLA. SEE NICHOLA.

NICOLAS. SEE NICHOLAS.

NICOL (ALSO NICOLE)

A confused young girl called Nicol
Went out on the field to bowl.
She hit the off stump
With a satisfying thump,
Then excitedly cried out, "Goal!"

NICOLETTE

There was an old lady – Nicolette,
Who examined me through her lorgnette.
With a ghost of a sneer,
She assumed a veneer,
Then said words I'd rather forget.

NIEL. SEE NEAL.

NIGEL

A famous old man called Nigel
Went out of his way to oblige all.
But he just couldn't cope
With his new telescope,
When watching the bright star Rigel.

NIKKY. SEE NICKKI.

NILES

There was a young artist called Niles –
And men hated his rough profiles.
They said that his skill
Was run-of-the-mill,
And he gave all his sitters stupid smiles.

NINA

There was a young dancer called Nina
Who danced in the city of Medina.
She would do an arabesque
That was so picturesque –
She became quite the best ballerina.

NINETTE

There was an old aunt called Ninette
Who was most strict on etiquette.
If you ate peas with a knife,
Or were rude to your wife,
She'd write to the local gazette.

NINIAN

There was a young man called Ninian
Who I employed as a do-it-all minion.
He said he was bright
At putting things right –
But that was just his opinion.

NOAH

There was an old man called Noah
Who sailed his ark to Goa.
It still lacked black bears
And some Indian hares,
But most of all – protozoa.

NOEL

There was a young person called Noel
Who said to a friend, "Oh hell!
Things have gone wrong.
What I sold for a song
Was not my own for bestowal."

NOLL

A budding MP called Noll
Came last but one in the poll.
He was after Lord Sutch[94]
(Which is not saying much),
But some people found it most droll.

NOLLIE (ALSO NOLLY)

There was a young gunner called Nollie
Who was told to fire off a volley.
He said, "I won't complain,
But it looks like rain,
I rather think this is sheer folly."

NORA (ALSO NORAH)

A naïve young girl called Nora
Once declared the heavens were for her.
I explained in vain
Again and again
That what she saw was the aurora.

---

[94] Lord Sutch: Screaming Lord Sutch of The Monster Raving Looney Party. He was a candidate in many British parliamentary elections.

NOREEN

There was a brash girl called Noreen
Whose behaviour was quite unforeseen.
She wore hot pants
To a ballroom dance
That was attended by the queen.

NORM

I once knew a schoolboy called Norm
Whose expulsion caused quite a storm.
Now I must confess
That I couldn't care less,
For he disrupted things in my form.

NORMA

An impulsive young girl called Norma
Once screamed that I never did warn her.
I had said, "Wait a tick!"
But she was too quick
And had jumped into a rather hot sauna.

NORMAN

A Latter-Day Saint called Norman
Became a very keen Mormon.
He said a polygamous life
With more than one wife,
Was better than being a doorman.

NUR

A whiskered old man called Nur
Had a face all covered in fur.
I had my suspicion
Of his composition
When he started to miaow and to purr.

NYE

There was young artist called Nye
Who was alleged to have a very good eye.
I know it was said
That his shirts were red,
But what shade of puce was his tie?

NYREE

There was a young girl – Nyree
Who left New Zealand by sea.
When she said a pakaha[95]
Might like to take her
In hand, I said, "Yes, try me."

---

[95] Pakaha: Maori for a white man.

There once was an airman called Ozzie…

OCKY

There was a young rider called Ocky
Whose career looked distinctly rocky.
He tried to keep quiet
That his new special diet
Was not the right sort for a jockey.

OCTAVIA

A naughty young girl called Octavia
Was well known for her misbehaviour.
Then she met a lad
Who really was bad.
Now both are in need of a saviour.

ODETTE

An energetic girl called Odette
Wanted to get to Tibet.
She cycled to Spain,
Just missed her train,
And finished her journey by jet.

ODILE

There was a young climber, Odile,
Who must have had nerves of steel.
She'd climb up a rock
In just an old frock
And a crampon attached to one heel.

ODO

A cub reporter called Odo
Was sent to the Isle of Komodo.
His words were succinct:
"But you're extinct!"
When he ran right into a dodo.

OLAF

There was a statistician called Olaf
Who said, "I have just drawn a graph.
So now I can see
How a very small bee
Can cause such pain to a giraffe."

OLGA

There was a young Russian called Olga
Who was named after the river Volga.
The vicar didn't see
He had forgotten the "V",
Until she was just two weeks older.

OLIVE

There was a young child called Olive,
Who said she couldn't forgive.
"I wasn't quite ready
When a boy stole my teddy,
And now I just don't want to live."

OLIVER

There was an old man called Oliver
Who asked me what should 'e give 'er.
I said, "Who do you mean –
That ghastly Jean?
If so, find a fast-flowing river."

OLIVIA

There was a strange girl called Olivia,
Who posted herself to Bolivia.
But the postman discovered
The parcel uncovered,
And didn't know where to deliver 'er.

OLWYN

There was a strange girl called Olwyn
Who bought a brand new coal bin.
She told her bloke
It wasn't for coke,
But for her to keep her stole in.

OLYMPIA

An adolescent young girl called Olympia
Who, one could say, was simply a
Pain in the neck.
And she was by heck!
For I've never known anyone pimplier.

OMAR

There was a young surfer called Omar
Who tackled an enormous comber.
As we looked out to sea,
He was ecstatic with glee,
And we heard him shout, "It's all go, Ma!"

OONA (ALSO OONAGH AND OONAH)

There was a sailor girl called Oona,
Who said that she would much sooner
Have a week in Calcutta
With a raving young nutter,
Than another rough day in that schooner.

OPAL

An unlucky young girl called Opal
Got glued to a piece of copal.
When she came unstuck,
She was hit by a truck,
And fell upside-down in a nopal.[96]

---

[96] Nopal: a type of cactus.

OPHELIA

There was a blind girl, Ophelia,
Who said, "I can't see, but can feel yer.
I can tell from your lips
The size of your hips,
And whether you have haemophilia."

OPRAH

There was a young girl called Oprah
Whose trade was selling copra.
But she could sing like a lark
When alone in the park,
And parody songs from opera.

ORLANDA

A forthright young girl called Orlanda
Was well known for outspoken candour.
She once said, "You,
Are a silly old shrew!"
And received a fierce back-hander.

ORVILLE

There was a young chippy called Orville
Who worked in the local saw-mill.
For lunch he had chips
And asparagus tips
All smothered in domestic raw dill.

OSBERT

There was a young man called Osbert
Who said what a dead loss was Bert.
The latter replied
"You do so deride;
My pride – it really was hurt."

OSBORN (ALSO OSBORNE)

A pretentious young man called Osborn
Always insisted that he was born
To a foreign princess,
In an officers' mess,
And they'd smuggled him out at dawn.

OSCAR

There was a simple man called Oscar
Who was taken by a girl to see Tosca.
He said that the plot
Was not worth a jot,
And he wondered how much it had cost 'er.

OSMOND (ALSO OSMUND)

There was a gastronome called Osmond
Who went out with a dark-rooted blonde.
She was not good looking,
But because of her cooking,
Of her he became extremely fond.

OSWALD

There is a young fool named Oswald
Whose head was scratched and half bald
It seems that in Zion
He stroked a large lion –
And that was the time he got mauled.

OTILLIE

A girl of contrasts was Otillie
Whom some said was a bright frisky filly.
But she played silly games
And called you foul names
And did her own thing, willy nilly.

OTIS

There was a young schoolboy called Otis
Who asked what to learn by rote is.
I said, "Forget any passion
And repeat parrot fashion.
Then you'll also learn what to quote is."

OTTO

There was an old cook called Otto
Well-known for his special risotto.
He'd blend all the rice
With rum and mixed spice,
Which made all the diners quite blotto.

OWEN

There was an old soak called Owen
Who was always puffin' and blowin'.
He'd tell all and sundry
He'd return Easter Monday.
But didn't know where he was goin'.

OZ

A forgetful young man called Oz
Never knew quite where he was.
When we asked him why
He said with a sigh,
"I dunno. Perhaps just because!"

OZZIE (ALSO OZZY)

There once was an airman called Ozzie
And a very fine young pilot was 'e.
He could drink turtle soup,
And loop the loop,
While flying around in a Mozzie.[97]

---

[97] Mozzie: nickname for the World War II aircraft, the Mosquito.

P

There was a young tenor called Pavel...

PADDY

There was a young lad called Paddy
Who was told to play golf with his daddy.
At the very first tee,
He realised that he
Was there to act as the caddy.

PAIGE

A temperamental actress called Paige
Once flew into a terrible rage
She cried that the star
Had wrecked her repertoire –
But was careful to say this offstage.

PALEY

A callused young man called Paley
Had skin all brittle and scaly.
They said it was chronic
So gave him a tonic,
And told him to imbibe it twice daily.

PALM

A placid young man called Palm
Never did anyone harm.
But I wish that he would
At least do some good,
Like inventing a new tune for a psalm.

PALMIRA

A flaxen-haired girl called Palmira
Lived on the Italian Riviera.
Her long golden locks
Swept down to her socks.
But that wig cost all of her lira.

PAM

A crossword addict called Pam
Was solving a TOUGH anagram.
She said, "It OUGHT
To be quite short –
In fact should be money for jam."

PANDORA

A nature lover called Pandora
Became a distinguished explorer.
You have to admire her,
She went alone to the Sahara,
And found new species of flora.

PANSY

An innovative cook called Pansy,
Started flavouring her food with tansy.
But the bitter taste
Was a bit of a waste,
For it didn't take anyone's fancy.

PAOLA

There was an old woman called Paola,
Who said to the police, "I've a prowler!"
The police searched the ground,
But nothing was found
Except a small dog – what a howler!

PARK

There was a young zoo-man called Park
Who lost his right arm in the Ark.
He was given wrong facts
About the big cats
When persuading two lions to embark.

PARKER

A man of strange habits was Parker
For he used to eat only moussaka.
He found that his hair
Dropped out here and there,
While his skin got very much darker.

PARMELLA

Lady Chatterley's maid was Parmella
Who tripped as she went down the cellar.
She thought, *By gum!*
My last moment has come!
Then fell into the arms of old Mellor.

PARNELL

A boring young man called Parnell
Always had a long story to tell.
He went on for hours
About space flight to Mars.
Sometimes I wish him in hell.

PARR

A gambling man called Parr
Stood up and shouted "Hurrah!
I used only a pin.
Now I've a lottery win.
I'll just go and prop up the bar."

PARRY

There was a Scots soldier called Parry
Who was told the foe he should harry.
But the sight of his kilt
Made the enemy wilt,
And they decamped with all they could carry.

PATIENCE

There was a new wife called Patience
Who loathed her spouse's machinations.
D'ye know what she said,
A week after she'd wed?
"I've got one too many relations."

PATRIA

There was a podgy girl called Patria
Whose neighbour said, "How fat you are!"
She replied, "It's a fact
That you have no tact.
Which shows me just what a cat you are."

PATRICIA

There was a young climber called Patricia
Who fell into a very narrow fissure.
Her friend, a boy scout,
Could not pull her out,
So he sent for the local militia.

PATSY

There was a young child called Patsy
Who asked, "Tell me, how does a bat see?"
"Why, it emits a sound,
Then times its rebound.
They've adapted to their habitat. See?"

PATTI (ALSO PATTY AND PATTIE)

A beautiful young girl called Patti
Had clothes that were really quite natty.
She had lovely hair,
And a face so rare.
It's a pity she was ever so scatty!

PAUL

A flighty young man called Paul
Tripped up at fancy-dress ball.
He wanted to pose
In doublet and hose,
But his pride went after his fall.

PAULA

There was a strange girl called Paula
Who started to shrink and get smaller.
She went to a quack
Who put her to the rack;
And now she's very much taller.

PAULEEN (ALSO PAULINE)

There was a fast girl called Pauleen
Who painted her lips bright green.
She said, "Red says 'Whoa!'
Whereas green says 'Go!'
'Tis a spur, if you see what I mean."

PAULETTE

An animal lover – Paulette,
Once went for a walk in the wet.
She fell in a puddle
And got in a muddle,
So they carted her off to the vet.

PAULINA

A pernickety girl called Paulina
Would never eat cold semolina.
They disguised it with rice
Which she said was quite nice
But maintained a disapproving demeanour.

PAULINE. SEE PAULEEN.

PAVEL

There was a young tenor called Pavel
Who adored the works of Ravel.
He thought Shérazade
Was much too hard,
But found he could sing it quite well.

PEARCE (ALSO PIERCE)

A man keen on fencing was Pearce
Whose ploy was to look very fierce.
And his skill with the foil
Made opponents recoil
While instructors used tapes of his tierce.

PEARL

A refined young girl called Pearl
Declared she would marry an earl.
Her cherished ambition
Came to fruition.
Now life's just a long social whirl.

PEDRO

There was a young rider called Pedro
Who declared that he'd said, "Whoa!"
This explains why my horse
Took off down the course –
It thought the man had cried, "Go!"

PEG

A lanky young girl called Peg
Was much too long in one leg.
When she went through doors,
She crawled on all fours,
As if she was going to beg.

PELHAM

There was a young boxer called Pelham
Who knew many jokes and would tell 'em.
When he held the floor
Men made for the door,
For if they didn't laugh he'd just fell 'em.

PELTON

There was an old tailor called Pelton
Who used to sell coats made of melton.[98]
If the cloth lacked lustre,
He'd make a small duster
Or maybe a hassock to be knelt on.

PEN

There was a young tot called Pen
Who surfed the Net now and then.
He said, "Nothing's cuter
Than my new computer,
But I wish I could count up to ten."

PENELOPE

There was a young schoolgirl – Penelope,
Who said to her friend, "Well! Oh, gee!
I can now recite
Half the alphabet all right.
But what's after MNOP?"

PENNY

A rather dim girl called Penny
Had faults that were frequent and many.
They asked if I knew
Of a talent or two,
But I said she had none, not any!

---

[98] Melton: a stout cloth without a nap.

PENWYN

A man on a diet called Penwyn,
Was remarkably slender and thin.
He wasted away
Till came the day
There was nothing left but his grin.

PEPITA

There was a large girl called Pepita
Who sat down and we couldn't unseat her.
We hired a small crane,
But this was in vain
Till she reduced her girth by one metre.

PERCE

A rather quiet man called Perce
Always found it so hard to converse.
If we called him a nutter
He would start to mutter
Something that seemed like a curse.

PERCY

There was a young toper called Percy
Who walked all the way to Stogursey.
When he arrived there,
He drank all the beer,
So the locals showed him no mercy.

PERDITA

A delicious looking girl called Perdita
Had as a pet a young cheetah.
But this feline did grow
As cats do, you know,
And one day decided to eat her.

PEREGRIN

A very odd man called Peregrin
Once told me, "I'll live in a bin.
I'll emulate Diogenes
And eat stodgy cheese.
Or maybe beans on a pin."

PERICLES

A man with a cold – Pericles,
Gave vent to one enormous sneeze.
The resulting reaction,
Changed the weather a fraction,
And created a force two breeze.

PERKIN

A colour-blind man called Perkin
Used to wear a puce-coloured jerkin.
His neighbours would pay
To keep him away
And he said this was better than workin'.

PERNELL (ALSO PERNELLE)

A sleep-walking man called Pernell
Fell down a rather deep well.
We didn't lose hope
But sent down a rope
Cut from the local church bell.

PERRY

A fruit-picking girl called Perry
Once ate a strange-looking berry.
She was terribly ill
So they gave her a pill
Washed down with a very sweet sherry.

PERRY

A young naval man called Perry
Had a job as a royal equerry.
He tripped on his sword,
So they made him a lord
And captain of a cross-channel ferry.

PERTH

There was an old man called Perth
Who was extremely wide in the girth.
It seemed all wrong
When he waddled along,
For he looked like nothing on earth.

PET

A lively young girl called Pet
Learnt to fly a very fast jet.
She would dress in ermine,
And could design a gas turbine.
She came from a very county set.

PETA

There was a peach of girl called Peta
And I sure would like to meet her.
But they say that she
Will charge you a fee
Just for the chance to greet her.

PETE

There was a young farmer called Pete
Who grew radioactive wheat.
His ears of corn
Looked all forlorn
As they grew in reflected heat.

PETER

An optimistic man called Peter
Used to drive a small three-seater.
But it only held two,
And this was all due
To him being a gross over-eater.

PETRA

There was a young cook called Petra
Who always gave a little bit extra.
And after eats
She'd recite some Keats;
Or Wordsworth, Robert Burns, et cetera.

PETRONELLA

In days long ago, Petronella
Studied art with Sir Godfrey Kneller.
When asked, "What's he like?"
She got very uptight,
But said he was a very fine feller.

PETULA

A thirsty young girl called Petula
Was ever so slightly peculiar.
When we gave her strong drink,
It went down in a wink.
It was just like having to refuel her.

PHILADELPHIA

A sensible young girl – Philadelphia,
Said, "I sure would like to be wealthier,
But I'd lend my voice,
If I had a choice
To being so very much healthier."

PHILBERT

There was an old man called Philbert
Who said, "Please give me my pill, Bert.
With my ticker so weak,
I'll be up the creak.
It's a heart attack we have to avert."

PHILLIPPA

An intrepid young girl called Phillippa
Once rode on the Blackpool Big Dipper.
She said that the ride
Made her feel funny inside,
But perhaps it was the big breakfast kipper.

PHILLIDA

A toothless old girl called Phillida
Said that she was once a "millider".
I knew she was bats,
And had never made hats.
Perhaps she was a bit of a kidder.

PHILOMELA

There was a strong girl called Philomela
Who had something her friends wouldn't tell her.
I doubt if she knew
That we all cried, "Phew!"
When she arrived at a dance with her feller.

PHILOMENA

There was a young girl – Philomena,
Who said, "I wish I were leaner."
She took a new pill
Which made her quite ill.
But it worked. I know 'cos I've seen her.

PHOEBE

There was a young gardener called Phoebe
Who grew an extraordinary hebe.
This amazing plant
Got an RHS grant,
And she gave it away as a freebie.

PHYLLIS

A pretty young girl called Phyllis
Used to roam the hills with the gillies.
When given a gun,
She said, "This is no fun,
I'd rather be at home with my frillies."

PIA

A bird-loving girl called Pia
Once had a very tame rhea.[99]
It was always taught
To never drink port.
But instead to drink Tia Maria.

PIERCE. SEE PEARCE.

PIERS

There was a young man called Piers
Who had very sensitive ears.
He could hear the sound
Of a worm underground,
Or his neighbours saying their prayers.

---

[99] Rhea: a kind of South American flightless bird.

PIETY

A serious young girl called Piety
Always believed in complete sobriety.
Then came the day
She got carried away,
And behaved with some impropriety.

PILAR

A harp-playing girl called Pilar
Was taller than most by far.
With her head in the ceiling,
She would play with some feeling,
And give an encore on the Hindu sitar.

PIP

There was an old barman called Pip
Who could make a special egg flip.
He used a certain wine
He said was divine
And which gave the drink quite a nip.

PIPPA

A rather wet girl called Pippa
Liked to swim in the sea with Flipper.
She would hold on to a fin.
Then the dolphin would grin.
And playfully try to nip her

PLATO

A scientific farmer called Plato
Grew a very large square potato.
Despite a good try
It just wouldn't fry.
But he managed to sell it to NATO.

POLL

A young girl in Norway called Poll
Unexpectedly encountered a troll.
A calm as could be,
She climbed up a tree
Took out a flask and said, "Skol!"

POLLY

There was a careless Wren called Polly
Whose deeds were a continuous folly.
Once on a trip
To a new battleship,
She fired off a 16-inch volley.

POLYANNA

There was a weird girl called Polyanna
Who had a very unfortunate manner.
This enraged her classmates,
Who shut the school gates
And implored the master to ban her.

POMONA

An astronomer girl called Pomona
Was known as a bit of a loner.
When on the Mendips
She studied the eclipse,
Especially the solar corona.

POPPY

A cub reporter called Poppy
Ran out of ideas for copy.
At last inspiration came,
But 'twas an awful shame
The editor read it and said, "Sloppy!"

PORTIA

A rash young woman called Portia
Was introduced to Lucretia Borgia.
Things started to blur
After dining with her
And she found she suffered from nausea.

POSY

An odd-looking girl called Posy
Had a future that looked quite rosy.
With a proboscis and brains
She became an expert on drains.
It was an advantage to be a bit nosey.

PRENTICE (ALSO PRENTISS)

I have a young tenant called Prentice
Who they say is *non compos mentis*.
He passes the time
Finding words that rhyme
But he cannot recall what his rent is.

PRESCOTT

There was an archaeologist called Prescott
Who wanted to travel to Mespot.[100]
He said he'd disembark
Somewhere in Iraq,
But he couldn't – because of that despot.

PRIMROSE

An Amazonian warrior – Primrose,
Had no friends and lots of grim foes.
She'd split them in twain
Again and again,
Then lay them all out in trim rows.

---

[100] Mespot: an abbreviation for Mesopotamia, an ancient region of southwest Asia.

PRINCE

There was a brash man called Prince
Who'd say things that might make me wince.
And added to that,
If he loathed your hat,
He'd pass some very broad hints.

PRISCA

There was a young traveller called Prisca
Who went red when they wanted to frisk her.
But they didn't twig
Till they removed her wig,
And found just a solitary whisker.

PRISCILLA

A beautiful maiden called Priscilla
Had suitors who all tried to thrill her.
As part of a stunt,
A pilot did a bunt –
Right over her luxury villa.

PROCTOR

A medical student called Proctor
Lived with the tribe called Choctaw.
He set their bones
And answered their phones,
And was made a sort of witch doctor.

PRU (ALSO PRUE)

Said a young lady called Pru,
"This really cannot be true!
I broke the rules,
Scooped all the pools,
And won the lottery too."

PRUDENCE

Said a rather broke pupil called Prudence,
"I'd like to meet some nice male students.
They must be quite liberal
And not too subliminal,
And kind enough to lend a few cents."

PRUDI (ALSO PRUDY)

There was an American Scot called Prudi,
Who felt she should do her "doody".
She devised a plan
To rejoin her clan,
Then buy a dirk and be feudy.

PRUE. SEE PRU.

PRUNELLA

A budding young actress – Prunella,
Was eager to play Cinderella.
In the interview room,
They gave her a broom
And said, "Start by sweeping the cellar!"

PRUNELLE

When I shared a meal with Prunelle
She finished up being unwell.
I wouldn't stoop
To blaming her soup,
But I too was feeling like hell.

PSYCHE

The beloved of Eros called Psyche
Was lucky to run into Tyche.[101]
They arranged to meet
On the morrow in Crete
To dish up the dirt with old Nike.[102]

PURITY

A rich young heiress called Purity
Was always kept at home for security.
But she loved the moors
And the great outdoors,
So fled when she reached maturity.

---

[101] Tyche: Greek mythology: the goddess of fortune.

[102] Nike: the Greek goddess of victory.

Q

There was a young camper called Quentin...

QUEEN

There was a young Wren called Queen
Who woke in a submarine.
She said, "I fell asleep
In the back of a jeep,
So where on earth have I been?"

QUENT

A man in a time-warp called Quent
Came back as soon as he went.
He said, "Life's a maze
And I'm in a haze,
So why on earth was I sent?"

QUENTIN

There was a young camper called Quentin
Who lacked space to put his tent in.
He had to revert
To a "want ads" advert,
But only one answer was sent in.

QUINN

There was a young driver called Quinn
Whose car was made out of tin.
He went for a drive
But failed to arrive,
For the chassis was much too thin.

QUINTIN

There was a brash man called Quintin
Whom girls said was always hintin'.
When they said they'd complain,
He did it again,
But silently – by winkin'.

R

A computer fan called Ramon…

RAB

There was a young hunk called Rab
Who had the gift of the gab.
Even when walking,
He never stopped talking.
But ladies thought he was fab.

RABBIE

There was a young boy called Rabbie
Who tended to be rather shabby.
But he went to college,
Learnt all the "knowledge",[103]
Then got a job as a cabby.

RACE

There was a fat man called Race
Who took up a great deal of space.
The cause of his size
Was – no exercise!
But I wouldn't say that to his face.

RACHEL (ALSO RACHELLE)

A pedantic young girl called Rachel
Declared that the letter H shall
Be truly aspirated –
Or it would be fated
To be sent to a sort of aitch hell.

RADLEY

A bit of a swank was Radley
For he never did anything badly.
But then he took a course
On doing the waltz.
That was his undoing – sadly.

---

[103] Knowledge: the information upon which London taxi drivers are tested before they can be licensed.

RADNOR

There was an old gourmand called Radnor
Who always overate and had more.
In competitive eating
He took quite a beating,
His opponent had just a tad more.

RAE (SEE ALSO RAY AND REY)

A young Scottish girl called Rae
Found a job in old Tannockbrae.
She got the position
On just one condition –
But what that was I won't say.

RAFAEL

A lonely young man called Rafael
Sailed away to a deserted isle.
He lived in two huts,
Ate shellfish and nuts,
And developed a hermit-like style.

RAFE (ALSO RALPH)

A strange young man called Rafe
Had shoes that began to chafe.
He inserted some rocks
Inside both his socks,
And said, "That's a lot better I vouchsafe."

RAFF

There was a young airman called Raff
Who made an enormous gaff.
He told an Air Marshal
That he was really quite partial
To eating peas off a knife in a caff.

RAINA

An aristocratic young girl called Raina
Once used a faulty tea strainer.
But she hit the ceiling
When she choked on Darjeeling.
I had quite a job to restrain her.

RAINE

There was a young sailor called Raine
Who set off for the Spanish Main.
But she lost her sail
In a terrible gale,
And her language became very profane.

RAISSE

There was a young girl called Raisse
Who just couldn't stand the pace.
She said, "I'm a failure,
I'm off to Australia,
'Cos there I'll have much more space."

RALPH (WHEN PRONOUNCED RAFE) SEE RAFE.

RAMA

A snappy old woman called Rama
Said I was creating a drama.
I had asked, "Top or bottom?
Was it woollen or cotton?"
When she cried that she'd lost one pyjama.

RAMON

A computer fan called Ramon
Bought a new CD with a game on.
But he forgot from which store,
And when the disk had a flaw,
He had no one to go to to claim on.

RAMONA

There was a young beauty called Ramona
Who was given a new bottle of toner.
But there were great ructions
When she lost the instructions,
And she blamed it all on the donor.

RAMSEY

There was a young Aussie called Ramsey
Whose name for his mother was "Mamsey".
But this caused sniggers
Among tough Oz diggers,
Who said to his face, "You're a pansy!"

RANA

An animal-loving girl called Rana
Had for a pet an iguana.
She said, "What a muddle,
It's so hard to cuddle,
And it only eats mashed up banana."

RANDA

An animal lover called Randa
Once owned a small giant panda.
It smoked cheroots
And ate bamboo shoots
That were flavoured with oleander.

RANDAL (ALSO RANDALL)

There was a young upstart called Randal
The cause of a notorious scandal.
When he danced at the Ritz,
His made-up tie came to bits
And they called him a sartorial vandal.

RANDOLF (ALSO RANDOLPH)

There was a young Captain called Randolf
Whose hobbies were bowling and golf.
We thought him quite balmy
When he rejoined the army,
But his handicap was one in the Gulf.

RANGER

Full of derring-do was Ranger
Who put himself in some danger.
He dived in a lake
To retrieve a cream cake –
There can't be many deeds stranger.

RANIA

There was a young girl called Rania
Who said she'd once met Titania.[104]
She claimed that this queen
Had wed Oberon unseen,
And had really preferred Urania.[105]

RANSOM

There was an old man called Ransom
Who once had a ride in a hansom.
But Turpin, known as Dick,
Got on board by a trick
And held the poor man up for ransom.

---

[104] Titania: the Queen of the Fairies.

[105] Urania: the muse of astronomy.

Ranulf

There was a young man called Ranulf
Who once played chess in the Gulf.
When his opponent said, "Check!"
He cried out, "Oh heck!
I'd be better off playing at golf."

Raoul

A pedantic young man called Raoul
Used to complain of that extra vowel.
"If I take out the O
And write it just so,
I'll save lots of ink. Here's how!"

Raquel

A brazen girl called Raquel
Once drank a large muscatel.
She mixed it with brandy
And a ginger beer shandy –
And I caught her just as she fell.

Rasha

A boastful young man called Rasha
Was known as a bold gatecrasher.
He claimed he was in Jordan,
His experience to broaden,
And had intruded on a do for Glubb Pasha.[106]

Raul

A dog-faced young man called Raul
Was wont to sit up and growl.
If they ever cried "Stop!"
He'd go over the top,
Get on his hind legs and howl.

---

[106] Glubb Pasha: Sir John Glubb, OC of the Arab Legion 1939-1956.

RAWLINS

There was a young man – Rawlins,
Whose wife gave birth to four quins.[107]
Or so it was stated
By a nurse who was sated
With a bottle of wine and four gins.

RAY (ALSO REY AND RAE)

There was a vain man called Ray
Whose hair went prematurely grey.
He sought to cure it
Or at least to obscure it,
But alopecia was coming his way.

RAY

There was a spiteful girl called Ray
Who promised to love and obey.
That horrible minx!
I know what she thinks –
That crossed fingers make it okay.

RAYBURN

Said a young actor called Rayburn,
"I have lines that I just won't learn.
I'll earn my wage,
By going on stage,
But I'll never ever do a gay turn."

RAYMOND

There was a young rambler called Raymond
Who fell in a dirty old pond.
He said, "Cor blimey!
I'm all black and slimy,
Now I'm in the slough of despond."

---

[107] Quins: quintuplets.

RAYMONDA

There was a young student called Raymonda
Who said that maths was beyond her.
When doing long division,
She was filled with indecision,
And wanted more time to ponder.

RAYMUND

A love-struck young man called Raymund
Always wore a red cummerbund.
To be quite specific,
It made him prolific,
Or could one not say – more fecund?

RAYNA

A conceited young model called Rayna
Started getting vainer and vainer.
She would twirl and pose
In new pantyhose,
Until someone decided to brain her.

RAYNOR

There was a young farmer called Raynor
Who wished that he could gain more.
It seemed that his crop
Would be quite a flop…
Unless, he declared, it would rain more.

REBA

An Arabian girl called Reba
Gave a pet to the Queen of Sheba.
It was hard to see
Being less than a flea,
And started as a single amoeba.[108]

---

[108] Amoeba: a tiny single-celled water creature that reproduces by dividing into two.

REBECCA

There was a wild girl called Rebecca
Who was known as a bit of a wrecker.
When in San Francisco,
She broke up a disco,
For the bouncer wasn't there to check her.

REDCLIFF

A strange-looking man called Redcliff
Was renowned for his curious red quiff.
He said it was created
By a bull he once baited,
Which charged him and gave him a head biff.

REDLEY

An aquatic young man called Redley
Took part in swimming medley.
His breaststroke was mediocre,
Like the way he played poker,
But his finishing crawl was quite deadly.

REDPATH

There was a young wizard called Redpath
Who mixed up potions in a red bath.
Into this he would put
Some limejuice and soot
And the hoof and horn from a dead calf.

REECE

A bony young man called Reece
Used to sit on the mantelpiece.
He said that his chair
Was much too bare,
But this gave a certain release.

REENA

A poor village girl called Reena,
Used to struggle to live as a gleaner.
One Halloween morn,
She went for the corn,
And since then no one has seen her.

REG

An irritating young man called Reg
Always ignored my home-grown veg.
Whenever he lunched
'Twas on nuts which he crunched,
And set all my teeth on edge.

REGGIE

An erudite young lad called Reggie
Was told to eat up his veggie.
He complained that tradition
Was never his ambition
And green things made him so edgy.

REGINA

There was a young girl called Regina
Who went on a slow ship to China.
When a typhoon blew,
It disabled the crew
And upturned that luxury liner.

REGINA (WHEN PRONOUNCED REGEENA)

There was a young Wren called Regina
Who had a very strange demeanour.
They said that her expression
Might cause some depression
And banned her throughout the marina.

REGINALD

An ignorant gem hunter – Reginald,
Once discovered a fine emerald.
He said it would be cruel
To surrender such a jewel,
Or whatever the darned thing was called.

REMUS

A pompous young curate called Remus
Told us he had come to redeem us
Although this was candid,
We thought it high-handed,
And said he'd better esteem us.

RENA

There was a grubby girl called Rena
Whom people said ought to be cleaner.
But she'd always glower
If we mentioned "shower",
And said we were trying to demean her.

RENATA

There was a plump girl called Renata
Who wore an enormous garter.
She said it represented
The fact that she'd consented
To marry the crown prince of Sparta.

RENE

An obstreperous man called Rene[109]
Was forever creating a scene.
For him it didn't suit
To lack the e acute,
And envy made him feel green.

---

[109] Obstreperous: turbulent, unruly, or noisy.

RENÉ

There was a young man called René
Who gained the admiration of many.
He once rowed to Timor
On the back of a door
And did it all for one penny.

RENITA

There was a young dancer – Renita
Who wanted to try the veleta.
In old London's Tower
She found a nice bower,[110]
And danced with a handsome beefeater.

RENNIE (ALSO RENNY)

A winter sportsman called Rennie
Who off went skiing one day when 'e
Hit some soft snow,
And in half a mo
Caused consternation to many.

RESEDA

A blushing young girl called Reseda
Asked a young man to wed her.
He said, "It ain't etiquette
For you to ask – yet."
Which made her very much redder.

REUBEN (ALSO RUBEN)

A student of Spanish called Reuben
Was determined to become a Cuban.
In the accustomed manner,
He applied in Havana,
But his accent left them all fumin'.

---

[110] Bower: a secluded place, especially in a garden; an arbour.

REVA

A young cloth-maker called Reva
Was taken on a job as a weaver.
But her fingers got caught
In the weft and the warp,
And had to be cut free with a cleaver.

REX

A new young sailor called Rex
Entangled a long piece of flex,
Which was rather imprudent
For a nautical student,
So they put him to washing the decks.

REXANA

In Bombay, a young girl called Rexana
Sought to achieve the state of nirvana.
She thought that some bliss
Would be achieved with a kiss,
Perhaps from a member of *varna*.[111]

REXFORD

There was a young man called Rexford
Who conveniently came from Wexford.
It makes it less hard
For a prospective old bard
When the only near rhyme is "next ford".

REY. SEE RAY OR RAE.

---

[111] Varna: a Hindu caste.

REYNARD

A precocious young man called Reynard
Once met a young girl – a Spaniard.
He said, "Oh, Señorita,
I vow there is none sweeter…"
But she thought his approach a canard.

RHAINE

There was a brazen girl called Rhaine
Who stripped for financial gain.
One day in a bar
She went just too far,
And they did not invite her again.

RHEA

A courageous young girl called Rhea
Said to herself, "Oh, dear!
I've climbed a giant sequoia
And now have paranoia,
And something of which I'm not clear."

RHETA (SEE ALSO RITA)

There was a young rider called Rheta
And no horse was known to defeat her.
Till one day in Rotten Row
She shouted out "Oh, whoa!"
And her horse reared up to unseat her.

RHETT

A rich young man called Rhett
Aspired to fly a fast jet.
He had enough wealth,
But they checked on his health,
Then said, "Maybe, but not yet."

RHODA

A travel agent called Rhoda
Drank lots of whisky and soda.
She then made a slip
When arranging a trip.
And booked a priest into a pagoda.

RHONA

There was a large girl called Rhona,
A quite exceptional blood donor.
When they extracted her gore
It was kept in a store.
If they wanted more they'd just phone her.

RHONDA

There was pretty girl called Rhonda
Whose hair just got blonder and blonder.
When it reached pure white,
It reacted with light,
And now she's a star way out yonder.

RHYANN

There is a young dancer called Rhyann
And no one can waltz like she can.
But she once took a risk,
When doing a whisk,
Which led to her having a knee scan.

RHYS

An unwilling young conscript called Rhys
Once covered himself with grease.
It was quite a good try,
But was pie in the sky,
And they never gave him his release.

Ria

There was a car owner called Ria
Who always drove around in first gear.
It seems that her clutch
Was not up to much
But quite why was not very clear.

Riannon

There was a young priest called Riannon
Who found a new use for a fanon.[112]
He polished a pew
He said, "With a view
To being short-listed for canon."

Riba

An elegant young girl called Riba
Was a cousin of the Queen of Sheba.
She had such prestige
And noblesse oblige
That everyone wanted to see her.

Rica

There was a silly girl called Rica
Who drank from a poisoned beaker.
She lost most of her weight
At an alarming rate,
And was sacked from her job as a streaker.

---

[112] Fanon: a cloth for handling holy vessels, etc.

RICARDA

There was a young girl – Ricarda,
Who was given a course at RADA.[113]
She found that acting
Was very exacting,
And said she'd never worked harder.

RICHARD

A Somerset man called Richard
Was terribly aged and whiskered.
He claimed he was alive
In nineteen-oh-five,
And had never in his life quit Chard.

RICK

There was a young thief called Rick
Who spent most of his time in the nick.
He once tried to steal
A lock from the Bastille;
He was incredibly thick.

RICKIE (ALSO RICKY)

There was a leg puller called Rickie
Who was always taking the mickey.[114]
By way of rebuttal,
We filled his coal scuttle
With things that were ever so sticky.

---

[113] RADA: Royal Academy of Dramatic Art.

[114] "Taking the mickey": making fun of people.

RIDER (ALSO RYDER)

> There was a young toper called Rider
> Who found a whole barrel of cider.
> After drinking pints galore,
> He reached his front door,
> And slurred, "Why don't they make these things
>   wider?"

RIDLEY

> Said a man from the bush called Ridley
> "I like this liver and kidney.
> Too right and it's true,
> It's better than 'roo,
> I'll up sticks and move into Sydney."

RIGG

> There was an old man called Rigg
> Who thought bald pates *infra dig*.
> But he got alopecia
> When he met a young Geisha.
> So now he goes around in a wig.

RILEY (ALSO RYLEY)

> There was a smooth talker called Riley
> Who thought of himself quite highly.
> When working abroad
> He was caught in a fraud –
> So perhaps he wasn't so wily!

RILLE

> There was a contralto called Rille
> Whose voice was ever so shrill.
> She once sang high C,
> When stung by a bee,
> Which she reached with a breathtaking trill.

RILETTE

There was a young WAAF called Rilette
Who stood too near a ramjet.
It singed her hair,
And bits here and there
That she'd mostly like to forget.

RISA

There was a young purist called Risa
Who went to the tower of Pisa.
She said, "It's not straight,
That's something I hate!"
And outraged Italians cried, "Seize her!"

RISLEY

There was a young girl called Risley
Who went off to shoot at Bisley.
When she heard the word "Pull!"
She hit a magpie and a bull.
But real ones, not the target – that's grisly!

RITA (SEE ALSO RHETA)

A foolish young girl called Rita
Took a candle to check the gas heater.
Too late she smelt gas,
Which exploded en masse,
And the floor came up halfway to greet her.

RIVA

A girl from the woods called Riva
Just wanted to tame a young beaver.
But that critter said, "Scram!
I'll go build me a dam.
Keep away or I'll give you swamp fever."

RITCHIE

An elephant man called Ritchie
Complained that he felt quite itchy.
On the seat of his howdah,
I'd dropped itching powder –
Some people say I'm quite bitchy!

ROALD

There was a young seaman called Roald
Who woke up one day with a cold.
He gave such a sneeze,
That it caused a strong breeze
Which blew him into the hold.

ROANNA

A computer girl called Roanna
Once put a new page in her scanner.
But the cartridge of ink
Developed a kink,
And leaked in the customary manner.

ROARK

There was a young poet called Roark
Whose car broke down in the dark.
He composed a rude sonnet
When he opened the bonnet
And found that the plugs had no spark.

ROB

A ministry man called Rob
Had the most extraordinary job.
He had to sing psalms
In organic farms
Before testing corn on the cob.

ROBBY

There was a young pilot called Robby
Who wanted to glide as a hobby.
He got somewhat miffed
When he found no slope lift,
And he landed on top of a bobby.

ROBERT

There was a kitchen cleaner called Robert
Who donned his very best job-shirt.
With the aid of a scraper
And some coarse sandpaper
He went off to take off some hob dirt.

ROBERTA

A spotty young girl called Roberta
For tea used to eat one Frankfurter.
It was with some disquiet
That I reviewed her diet,
And went out of my way to convert her.

ROBERTO

There was a young composer called Roberto
Who wrote a new piano concerto.
He made improvements
To all the three movements,
Which were *allegro*, *vivace* and *scherzo*.

ROBIN

A man of many parts was Robin
Who had an old horse called Dobbin.
He earned his keep
By transporting sheep,
And the rest of the time by odd-jobbin'.

ROBIN (ALSO ROBYN)

> Said a flirtatious young girl called Robin,
> "My heart is always a-throbbin'.
> It affects the men,
> Whom I see now and then,
> And others with whom I'm hobnobbin'."

ROBINA

> There was a young dancer – Robina,
> Who wished to be a ballerina.
> But she didn't want
> To dance à pointes,
> And was banned for that misdemeanour.

ROBYN. SEE ROBIN.

ROCK

> There was an unusual man called Rock
> Whom most of us tended to mock.
> But we explained that the reason
> Was tied to the season:
> For in summer he wore a girl's frock.

ROCKY

> A greedy young man called Rocky
> Was the fastest eater of gnocchi.
> But he had quite a job
> To eat corn on the cob,
> Which stopped him from getting too cocky.

ROD (ALSO RODD)

> A laconic young man called Rod,
> Would never say "Yes", but just nod.
> But wouldn't you know
> He did the same for "No";
> He really was a bit odd.

RODRICK

There was a young builder called Rodrick
Who'd be pleased to show us the hod trick.[115]
He'd give it a spin
On the end of his chin,
And never did drop the odd brick.

RODGER. SEE ROGER.

RODNEY

There was a weird man called Rodney
Whom people said was ungodly.
He did prestidigitation[116]
Plus a form of meditation,
And he went about things most oddly.

ROGER (ALSO RODGER)

There was an old man called Roger
Known to some as an elderly codger.
But when work was around
He couldn't be found,
And became known as the artful dodger.

ROLAND

There was a young man called Roland
Who went on a short trip to Poland.
He saw a great potential
For the not inconsequential,
And thought it was a get-up-and-go land.

---

[115] Hod: a V-shaped open trough on a pole used for carrying bricks, mortar, etc.

[116] Prestidigitation: an act of conjuring.

Rolf

There was a young Aussie called Rolf
Who said he'd never played golf.
He could play a didgeridoo,
And paint like you-know-who
But he couldn't sink a putt like Rudolf.

Rollo

A man with a thirst was Rollo
Who liked to take a bath and just wallow.
If just a little tug
Didn't move the rubber plug,
He'd empty the bath with one swallow.

Roma

A nouvelle riche girl called Roma
Always smelt of a strange aroma.
For one day in Nice
She found ambergris,[117]
While working as the local beachcomber.

Romelle

There was a saucy girl called Romelle,
A pert little mademoiselle.
She said that etiquette
Was not for her – yet.
Which was, perhaps, just as well.

Romeo

There was an old man called Romeo
Who went to the Millennium Dome-eo.
At the end of the day,
He said, "It's okay,
And now I'm back to my home-eo."

---

[117] Ambergris: a valuable substance used in the making of perfume.

RON

There was a young farmer called Ron
Who owned a very large swan.
When it landed on ice
It broke through in a trice
And in the wink of an eye it was gone.

RONA

An RSPA girl called Rona
Once paid a visit to Barcelona.
At a bullfight she cheered
When a matador got speared,
And was expelled as a *persona non grata*.

RONALD

There was a desperate man called Ronald
Who exclaimed that he'd just gone bald.
He used a giant pourer
To put on hair restorer
But his scalp changed hue to dun-gold.

RONALDA

A hard-to-please girl called Ronalda
Declared that I no longer wowed her.
She claimed that I fussed
About her thick dust.
And she abhorred my talcum powder.

RONAN

A conceited young man called Ronan
Stated that he was afraid of no man;
"But I can't bear snakes,
Manglewurzles and cakes,
And very few people that I know can."

Ronnie

There was a clever man called Ronnie,
Known as a come-lately Johnny.
Despite being arthritic,
And almost paralytic
He made some really big money.

Ronson

A silly young man called Ronson
Once climbed up a grey-coloured sponson.
But he almost fainted
When he found it newly-painted
And it was nearly to be his swansong.

Rooney

There was a young student called Rooney
Who took a short course at uni.
He read some chronometry,
And then trigonometry,
But stopped when they made him feel puny.

Roper

There was an old barfly called Roper
Who became a notorious toper.[118]
He once caused a collision,
With his cross-eyed double-vision
And became a forlorn no-hoper.

Rory

A young raconteur called Rory
Knew how to tell a good story.
His output was prolific
And his income terrific.
If only his tales weren't so gory!

---

[118] Toper: someone who drinks alcohol to excess; an alcholic.

ROS (ALSO ROZ)

A vague young girl called Ros
Went off to the land of Oz.
When we asked her why,
She just said, "Oh, fie!
I don't know, I s'pose it's just 'cos."

ROSA

A dotty young girl called Rosa
Once put to me a very fine poser.
"If a powerful back hoe
Has quite so much go,
Why do they call it a bull*dozer*?"

ROSALIN (ALSO ROSALYN)

A spoilt young sailor – Rosalin,
Had but scant discipline.
On a well-known occasion
And with no one's persuasion,
She stole a yacht for some sailin'.

ROSALIND

There was a young Wren – Rosalind,
Who sailed too close to the wind.
When her boat became inverted
She wasn't disconcerted,
She came to the surface and grinned.

ROSALINDA

A young island girl – Rosalinda,
Once ran short of essential tinder.
I tried hard to help
By supplying dried kelp
But she declared it would only hinder.

Rosaline

A budding young actress – Rosaline,
Could only just count up to nine.
She would rather read dramatics
Than study mathematics.
And anyway, who was Einstein?

Rosalyn. See Rosalin.

Rosamund

A bouncy young girl called Rosamund
Was small and very rotund.
And one's eye was diverted
If not disconcerted
By the length of her cummerbund.

Rosamunda

A girl from the north – Rosamunda,
Disappeared during a walk in the tundra.
She was looking for mosses
To feed her poor hosses,
And they found her half a foot under.

Rosanne

A dozy young girl called Rosanne
Claimed she had an oh-so-cunning plan.
She would divert the Gulf Stream
And use the surplus steam.
(White coats took her away in a van.)

Roscoe

There was a nice man called Roscoe
Who was really a dead loss tho',
I'm forced to say,
That he had had his day,
He might be gifted – not as a boss tho'.

ROSE

There was a young musician called Rose
Who struck an unconventional pose.
She would always kneel
When she played the glockenspiel,
Which she did with one of her toes.

ROSELLE

A girl of some girth was Roselle
And she had a voice like a bell.
But I'll come clean,
It was like Big Ben, I mean,
And she acted as town crier as well.

ROSEMARY

There was a blue stocking – Rosemary,
Whose outlook was shockingly merry.
She amazed her tutor
By riding a scooter
Up the gangplank of the Gosport ferry.

ROSEMOND

There was a naïve girl – Rosemond,
Who was told to bathe in a pond.
I said it was crude
To bathe in the nude;
She agreed but said she'd been conned.

ROSENE

There was a fiery girl called Rosene
Who jumped on to a trampoline,
When others did scoff,
She bounced right off
And on them vented her spleen.

ROSETTE

There was a new cook called Rosette
Whose potatoes were always noisettes.
I told her, "Try boiled!"
From which she recoiled
And said they made her upset.

ROSIE (ALSO ROSY)

There was a young author called Rosie
Whose books sounded ever so prosy.
She thought what might suit her
Was a course with a tutor,
But that was no good, he was dozy.

ROSINA

There was a new baby – Rosina;
And my job as a nurse was to clean her.
I'm ready to swear.
It didn't stop there;
In the end my job was to wean her.

ROSLIN (ALSO ROSSLYN)

A bewildered young girl called Roslin
Went out in her car for a spin.
She drove to Miami,
Then murmured, "Oh damn me,
I've forgotten to pick up my twin."

ROSWELL

I once had a hero called Roswell
Whose words to me were just gospel.
If he said black was white,
I would claim he was right.
It was later I learnt he could josh well!

ROSY. SEE ROSIE.

ROTH

There was a young man called Roth
Who wrapped himself round with a cloth.
It was draughty in places
With some open spaces
Caused by the deeds of a moth.

ROVER

There was a young dancer called Rover
Who thought that he was in clover.
There was nothing false
About his perfect waltz.
And he won medals for his bossa nova.

ROWE

There was a young farmer called Rowe
Who said, "I must get rid of that dzo.[119]
It produces no milk,
Or stuff of that ilk,
And keeps stepping on to my toe."

ROWELL

A bearded old man called Rowell
Was invited to assist with Noël.
They put him indoors
As their new Santa Claus,
With gifts for his own bestowal.

---

[119] Dzo: a hybrid of a cow and a yak.

Rowena

An enterprising girl called Rowena
Took ship to old Argentina.
She went to Mar del Plata,
And ate a chipolata,
But since then no one has seen her.

Roxanna

I had a young girlfriend – Roxanna,
Who had an unpredictable manner.
If I asked for a hug,
She'd give a short shrug.
But a kiss? She'd shout "Hosanna!"

Roxanne

A talkative girl called Roxanne
Once said she could always fox Man.
"They are so naïve,
So what can they achieve?
In contrast to what a chatterbox can?"

Roxie (also Roxy)

There was a fast girl called Roxie
Who must have been somebody's doxy.[120]
If you thought it was me
How on earth could it be?
If she were it was all done by proxy.

Roxina

There was a young poet called Roxina
Who asked what could rhyme with "ina"?
But my ideas had run dry,
So she started to cry.
I tell you I've never felt meaner.

---

[120] Doxy: a lover or mistress.

ROXINE

There was a town girl called Roxine
Who said she had never a fox seen.
She looked near some strata,
But that was a non-starter.
Instead, she found pyroxine.[121]

ROXY. SEE ROXIE.

ROY

An enterprising lad called Roy
Was taken on as a new call-boy.
He said a benefactor
Could help him be an actor;
In the meantime this was a ploy.

ROYAL

A patriotic man called Royal
Once rolled himself up in some foil.
Then attached a flag
To a dirty old rag.
Just to prove he was loyal.

ROYCE

There was a young singer called Royce
Who gave us cause to rejoice.
He said he wouldn't cavil[122]
He just gargled with gravel,
And we enjoyed his lovely deep voice.

---

[121] Pyroxine: a component of igneus rock.

[122] Cavil: make petty objections.

ROYDON

There was an old man called Roydon
Who lived on the outskirts of Croydon.
He was quite young at heart,
But it wasn't so smart
When he took up with a fierce little hoyden.[123]

ROZ. SEE ROS.

ROZELLA

A budding young actress – Rozella,
Was keen to understudy Cinderella.
But it made her wince
When she saw the "prince",
Who had just broken out with rubella.

RUBE

There was an old man called Rube
Who said he had made a boob.
"I got into a muddle
And stepped in a puddle,
Now I can't find my way to the tube."

RUBEN. SEE REUBEN.

RUBETTE

There was a young tourist called Rubette
Who slept in a first class couchette.
When she finally reached Nice,
She felt like a piece
Of something she'd like to forget.

---

[123] Hoyden: a boisterous girl.

RUBEY (ALSO RUBY)

A generous young girl called Rubey
Was at heart just a rather big booby.
When she wore double As,[124]
She was going through a phase,
For her body was tall, thin and tubey.

RUDD

An idiot of a man called Rudd
Got caught up a tree in a flood.
When the waters receded,
No warnings were heeded,
And he fell to earth with a thud.

RUDY

There was a young man called Rudy
Whose buddies said he was no "beaudy".
They claimed that his mug
Resembled a jug,
And a Scot said he was ever so feudy.

RUELLE

There was a spiteful man called Ruelle
Whom friends thought was ever so cruel.
By way of revenge,
They went to Stonehenge,
And forcibly fed him with gruel.

RUFE

There was a priggish man called Rufe
Who was always rather aloof.
And if you stated a fact,
He'd say, without tact,
"What I want now is some proof."

---

[124] Double A: a bra size.

Rufina

There was a young dancer called Rufina –
A lithe and winsome ballerina.
And just for a dare,
She would bop on the pier,
Or waltz right along the marina.

Rufus

There was a young joker called Rufus
Who did his very best to spoof us.
He said an éclair
Was made from horsehair,
But this was too extreme to goof us.

Rula

There was a Hawaiian girl called Rula
Who was expert at dancing the hula.
She might have looked pert
When she swished her grass skirt,
But she did it to keep herself cooler.

Rule

An inventive young man called Rule
Claimed that he'd just seen a ghoul.
He seemed quite narked
When we just remarked,
"But you were ever the one to drool."

Rupert

A fawning young man called Rupert
Was always a bit of a flirt.
When he eyed my belle,
I said, "Go to hell!"
He replied, "Oh man, you do hurt!"

RUPERTA

There was a young student – Ruperta
Who liked all the writings of Goethe.
I thought I would kill her
When she started on Schiller,
Instead of trysting with me in Bizerta.

RUPERTO

There was a young musician Ruperto
Renowned 'cos he had such a queer toe.
It was red, black and brown,
And would beat up and down
In time to his latest concerto.

RUSH

A keen young gardener called Rush
Had a lawn so fertile and lush.
He made his wife
Cut the grass with a knife;
If she griped, he'd just tell her, "Shush!"

RUSS

A man with a hernia called Russ
Used to talk to it while on the bus.
One day it replied,
In words rude and snide,
"Why don't you get me a truss?"

RUSSELL

A fancy young man called Russell
Used to get dressed in a hustle.
As a quick-change artist,
He was always the fastest,
Till one day he tried on a bustle.

RUST

A man of few words was young Rust
Who learnt that his firm had gone bust.
When I asked for the reason,
He said, "It's the season;
But I'll tell you the rest if I must."

RUSTY

A perspiring young man called Rusty
Was thought to be handsome and lusty.
But the girls did a flit
When they got near this git
Saying, "Cor! He's ever so musty."

RUTH

There was a pretty girl called Ruth
Who would always tell the truth.
When I asked, "Are you mine?"
She said, "You're a swine,
And a bit too long in the tooth!"

RUTHIE

There was a blind date called Ruthie
Who they said was tall, thin and couthie.[125]
How I wish I'd missed
That carefully arranged tryst,
For her face was horsey and toothy.

RYAN

A depressed young man called Ryan
Spent most of his time a-sighin'.
His thoughts were so quixotic
That he became almost neurotic,
And spoke about nothing but dyin'.

---

[125] Couthie: (Scottish) friendly.

RYDER. SEE RIDER.

RYE

> There was a young pilot called Rye
> Who always flew extremely high.
> He said, "It's better than low,
> Or moderately slow,
> If I stall I've got the whole sky."

RYLAND

> There was a traveller called Ryland
> Who walked all the way to Thailand.
> But he made a faux pas,
> So did not get far
> When he tried to reach Bali by land.

RYLE

> There was a young bridegroom called Ryle
> Who always did things in great style.
> He was covered in dahlias
> And his bride wore azaleas,
> When they walked hand in hand down the aisle.

RYLEY. SEE RILEY.

S

A marathon runner called Sharon...

SABBY

A snooty young girl called Sabby
Once hailed a passing cabby.
But she let him pass by
For he wore quite the wrong tie
For dropping her off at the Abbey.

SABRINA

A brash young girl called Sabrina
Sat alone in a Spanish cantina.
She yelled, "¡Una paella por favor!"
Through a half-open door,
When no one appeared to have seen her.

SACHA

There was a young midget called Sacha
Who lived in a small Russian dacha.[126]
He didn't need a mansion,
Or room for expansion,
Because of his limited stature.

SACHA

A girl in a clinic called Sacha
Once tried an electric back-scratcher.
With reciprocating motion
And a good cleansing lotion,
There was no chiropractor to match her.

SADIE

There was an old woman called Sadie
Who no one could call a lady.
She was loud and coarse,
Without remorse,
And a background described as most shady.

---

[126] Dacha: a country house or cottage in Russia.

SAFFRON

Said a young service girl called Saffron,
"Shall we go into that little old caff, Ron?"
He replied, "Let's try the NAFFI
Which is run by a taffy,
He'll sell you a very good RAF bun."

SAL

An athletic young girl called Sal
Once walked on her hands down the mall.
And just for a dare,
In Trafalgar Square,
Climbed Nelson's Column with a pal.

SALINA

A vulgar young girl called Salina,
Once committed a small misdemeanour.
She told the lady mayor
She disliked her hair
And it resembled brown semolina.

SALLY

An exasperating girl called Sally
Was inclined to go and dilly-dally.
She once made me stop
Outside a jeweller's shop,
And I waited an hour in the alley.

SALLY ANN

There was a naïve girl – Sally Ann,
Who went out with an old tallyman.
She really swore blue murder
When he put her in purdah,
And vowed she'd escape the bally man.

SALOME

There was a young tourist called Salome
Who made a short trip to the Komi.[127]
She was put in a jacuzzi
All full of soap, and oozy,
And finished up naked but foamy.

SAM

There was a young chef called Sam
Who got sent out to Vietnam.
When he arrived in Hué,
They sent him away,
'Cos he couldn't cook eggs and ham.

SAMANTHA

There was a strange girl called Samantha
Who kept as a pet a shy panther.
If it scented danger,
Or spotted a stranger,
It would hide behind a giant pyrocantha.

SAMMY

There was an English teacher called Sammy
Who cleaned his car with a chamois.
While working he mused
How aliens get confused
When we pronounce "amois" like "ammy".

SAMMY

There was a young girl called Sammy
Who took herself off to Miami.
She thought that the Keys
Were just the bees' knees,
But the Everglades were ever so clammy.

---

[127] Komi: Finnish people.

SAMPSON (ALSO SAMSON)

A young postal worker called Sampson
Had no lick with which to glue stamps on.
Having no saliva
He used a screwdriver
To spoon sticky types of jams on.

SAMUEL

There was an old gardener called Samuel
Who grew an enormous biannual.
He used an expletive
And became quite secretive
When I asked for the name of his manual.

SANDIE (ALSO SANDY)

There was a young jockey called Sandie
Whose legs were short, thick and bandy.
But he always avowed
That he was so endowed
To make riding small horses more handy.

SARA

There was an old peeress called Sara
Who refused to wear a tiara.
She said it was fate
That gave her a bald pate,[128]
While the jewels emphasized her mascara.

SARAH

There's a zany young girl called Sarah
Who'll do queer things if you dare her.
She once trained a gannet
To fly round the planet,
And bomb the French Riviera.

---

[128] Pate: (archaic) the head.

SARAH JANE

There was a young cowgirl – Sarah Jane,
Who used to drive me insane.
It's not so groovy
To take her to a movie,
And then be told she hated John Wayne.

SASHA

There was a young soldier called Sasha
Whose deeds got more daring and rasher.
His last escapade
Was to rush on parade,
Rigged out in the attire of a flasher.

SASKIA

I once knew a girl called Saskia.
What a very odd name – well I ask yer!
It's enough to make a poet
Say, "Oh hell, I'll go and stow it."
Or entreat my friends, "I've a task for yer."

SCARLET (ALSO SCARLETT)

There was a young actress called Scarlet
Much famed for her role as a starlet.
But new lines on her face
Caused a fall from grace,
But she accepted the part of a varlet.[129]

SCOTT

A young millionaire called Scott
Once owned a luxury yacht.
He sailed to the Bahamas
Wearing silk pyjamas,
Anything else? Well, no, not a lot.

---

[129] Varlet: (archaic) a menial or rascal.

Scottie (also Scotty)

There was a young traveller called Scottie
Who went to the land of the zloty.[130]
But when in Warsaw
He fell foul of the law,
And the proceedings nearly drove him quite dotty.

Seamas (also Seamus)

There was a young actor called Seamas
A Shakespearean who was really quite famous.
When he played the part of Lear,
I would wipe away a tear,
For his orations quite overcame us.

Sean (also Shaun and Shawn)

There was a young artist called Sean
Who showed me some things he had drawn.
He'd done some cartoons
Of some of the goons,
And one of an amorous prawn.

Seb

There was a young swain called Seb
Who dated a glamorous deb.
But when she made eyes
At all the other guys,
His ardour just started to ebb.

Sebastian

There was a young sailor called Sebastian
Who went for a row on the Caspian.
Life became fraught
When he beached at a fort,
For they thought he was attacking their bastion.

---

[130] Zloty: the chief monetary unit of Poland.

SELENA

There was a chatty girl called Selena
Who told her life story to Ena.
But it's a woman's natural way
To tell a secret each day,
Which she does with a dead-pan demeanour.

SELWYN

There was an old man called Selwyn
Who built a log hut to dwell in.
He was digging a drain
When down came the rain,
And he slipped in the mud and fell in.

SERENA

There was a young girl called Serena
Who once ate a snitzel Wiener.
She had to cheat
By transposing the meat,
For snitzel doesn't rhyme with "eena".

SETH

There was a young student called Seth
Who always ran out of breath.
When down in the campus,
He'd sound like a grampus,
Especially when declaiming Macbeth.

SEYMOUR

There was young brave called Seymour
Who joined the tribe called Choctaw.
He bought skins from a Cree
And built a tepee,
Then tried to woo an old squaw.

SHANDY

There was a mad toper called Shandy
Who found a Swiss knife came in handy.
He cut out the shape
Of an over-sized ape,
Then tried to make it drink brandy.

SHANE

There was a young cowboy called Shane
Who found life was just too mundane.
So he bought a six-shooter,
And with the help of a tutor
Became the fastest gun on the plain.

SHANI (PRONOUNCED SHARNI)

A voluble girl called Shani
Once ate some chilli con carne.
She found it so hot
That she cried, "Great Scot!
That finally got rid of my blarney."

SHANI (PRONOUNCED SHAYNY)

A strange young girl called Shani
Always appeared brash and so zany.
But this was a ruse
Designed to confuse;
In fact she was really quite brainy.

SHARI

A lucky young trekker called Shari
Got lost in the Kalahari.
She lived on ripe mango
Growing by the Okavango,
And was found by a roving safari.

SHARMAINE. SEE CHARMAINE.

Sharon

A marathon runner called Sharon
Found the leaders were really far on.
She found fresh reserves
By eating preserves,
Which she enhanced by spreading choc bar on.

Sharron

There was a Scottish girl called Sharron
(The one with the extra R on).
She swam the river Clyde
Against a strong rip tide
For a tryst on the Isle of Arran.

Shaun. See Sean.

Shawn. See Sean.

Sheba

There was a young tourist called Sheba
Who went to the dam at Kariba.
With the chief's assent,
She spent the night in a tent,
Protected by a strong zareba.[131]

Sheela (also Sheila)

There was a sick girl called Sheela
Who was told of a gifted healer.
In Disneyland,
He held her hand.
Then she found he was a wheeler-dealer.

---

[131] Zareba: enclosure around African village.

SHEENA (ALSO SHEENAGH)

There was a young witness called Sheena
Who received a mysterious subpoena.
At half past three,
She was required to be
In a courtroom in Argentina.

SHEILA. SEE SHEELA.

SHELLY

An animal lover called Shelly
Always had fire in his belly.
But it was his fear of snakes
That gave him the shakes;
If he saw one his feet turned to jelly.

SHEM

A computer expert called Shem
Bought a state of the art modem.
Having put it in place,
He felt the disgrace
Of making a phone call to THEM.

SHERI (ALSO SHERIE)

A self-important girl called Sheri
Proclaimed she should have an equerry.
They cried, "That's illegal,
Unless you are regal,
So forget it and go and make merry."

SHERIDAN

There was a young student called Sheridan
Who was a very jolly and merry man.
He'd think up a hoax,
Or play lots of jokes,
Such as pouring out tea from a jerrycan.

SHERLEY (ALSO SHIRLEY AND SHIRLEE)

A pretty young girl called Sherley
Had hair that was ever so curly.
She said it was due
To her pa – a Sioux,
Who plaited her hair twice yearly.

SHIRL

A Hell's Angel's moll called Shirl
Possessed a lovely kiss curl.
But her hair went all fuzzy,
And she looked like a hussy
When she took her new bike for a whirl.

SHOLTO

There was a young cowboy called Sholto
Who made for the nearest bolthole.
He fought for his life
With just a penknife –
He wished that he'd worn his Colt tho'.

SIÁN (PRONOUNCED SHAHN)

A young Irish man called Sián
Claimed someone had spun him a yarn.
But she didn't goof
By accepting false proof,
He just curled her lip and said, "Garn!"

SIBIL (ALSO SYBIL)

A difficult young girl called Sibil
Was always inclined to scribble.
When we read her scrawl –
Just a part (not all) –
She said, "Do go away and don't quibble!"

SID (ALSO SYD)

A sensitive young man called Sid
One day did tread on a squid.
He said that the feeling
Was very revealing,
And it felt like a large arachnid.

SIDNEY (ALSO SYDNEY)

At an auction that awful man Sidney
Once claimed he could always outbid me.
At the very next sale
I let cunning prevail
And he mistakenly bid for a kidney.

SIEGFRIED (ALSO SIGFRIED)

There was a young pianist – Siegfried,
Who said he wanted to see Grieg.
He went to Belgravia
Instead of Scandinavia,
So he failed in his quest indeed.

SIGGY

There was a young man called Siggy
Who owned a small cat called Tiggy.
But its tremendous greed
Made it expensive to feed
So he changed its appellation to Piggy.

SILAS

There was a young artist called Silas
And I'm sure he was out to beguile us.
His art form was bizarre:
He'd take a cigar
And draw on the leaf with a stylus.

SILVESTER (ALSO SYLVESTER)

There was a financier called Silvester
Who was a brilliant city investor.
He was also an enigma
Who had this slight stigma:
After luncheon he took a siesta.

SILVIA (ALSO SYLVIA)

Said a psychic Met girl called Silvia,
"The deep depression's still there.
But I threw a dart
At my synoptic chart,
And it shows that the wind will veer."

SIM

A silly young man called Sim
Always liked to stand on the rim.
When he did this on Stromboli
And walked forward slowly,
His future prospects were grim.

SIMEON

There was a young chef called Simeon
Who liked to put his new pinny on.
He'd then make scrambled egg,
With some salt and nutmeg,
But never did think to gimme one.

SIMMIE

A young entertainer called Simmie
Would always belly dance with a shimmy.
But it spoilt the show
When we got up to go,
For she advanced with a bowl and said, "Gimme!"

SIMON

A man from Athens called Simon
Went off to dine with old Timon.
But that misanthrope
Was watching a soap,
And told him to go find his pieman.

SIMONA

An enigmatic looking girl called Simona
Arrived in Bergen with no krone.
After a night and a day,
They sent her away,
Expelled as a *non grata persona*.

SIMONE

A vociferous girl called Simone
Was always on the telephone.
At the end of a year,
She was in despair,
For she'd grown an extra cheekbone.

SINCLAIR

There was a young fool called Sinclair
Who entered a lion's den for a dare.
The beast said, "You've a nerve,
I've had my hors d'oeuvres,
And I like my meat cooked, not rare."

SINDY. SEE CINDY.

SINEAD (PRONOUNCED SHIN-ADE)

A muddled young girl called Sinead
Was a difficult one to persuade.
She said that Fahrenheit
Gave her frostbite;
She'd rather have Centigrade.

SIOBHAN (PRONOUNCED SHI-VORN)

There was a loud girl called Siobhan,
With a voice like a ship's foghorn.
In Zermat her whisper
Sounded much crisper,
But could be heard up the Matterhorn.

SIS. SEE CIS.

SISSIE. SEE CISSY.

SISSY. SEE CISSY.

SKEETER

An enterprising man called Skeeter
Had his very own traffic meter.
For a coin in the slot,
You reserved a spot,
And could also buy soup by the litre.

SOL

A surveyor for maps called Sol
Placed a trig point down in a col.
His boss went berserk,
And said, "You're a berk!
You confused the darned thing with a knoll."

SOLLY

A glum-looking man called Solly
Was thought by all to be a wally.
But I took them to task
For behind the mask
I knew he was sharp and quite jolly.

SOLOMON

An ambitious young man called Solomon
Was keen on becoming a dollar man.
He went quite demented
Over things he'd invented,
But he retired as a rich white-collar man.

SOMERSET

A percussion man called Somerset
Was keen to get a new drummer set.
But he was full of pique
When his rad sprang a leak,
So instead had to buy a new plumber set.

SONIA (ALSO SONJA AND SONYA)

There was a pretty girl called Sonia,
And I've never seen anyone bonnier.
But looks are deceptive
If one's not perceptive.
So take great care or she'll con yer.

SONNIE (ALSO SONNY AND SUNNY)

There was a young comic called Sonnie
Who loved to use words that were punny.
It mattered not a jot
Whether they rhymed or not,
So long as he thought they were funny.

SOPHIA

A slightly deaf girl called Sophia
Once complained I'd called her a liar.
I could have died!
"You misheard!" I cried,
"I said, 'In the hall was your lyre.'"

SOPHIE (ALSO SOPHY)

There was a young girl called Sophie
Who sang the song called the strophe.[132]
The words were naughty,
But were sung with such forte
That they won the Athenian trophy.

SPENCER

A bright young man called Spencer
Was a boxer as well as a fencer.
He could use the sabre
Or toss a caber,
And was a founder member of Mensa.

SPIKE

An enterprising man called Spike
Once found a hole in a dyke.
He put in some gum
Rammed home with his thumb,
And this caused a trade union strike.

SPRING

A young eastern girl called Spring
Knew all about yang and ying.
She said that yang[133]
Gave her a bang,
While ying gave her plenty of zing

---

[132] Strophe: in a Greek play the song sung by the chorus as it moved towards one side.

[133] Ying and Yang: the two opposing and complementary principles of Chinese philosophy, religion, and medicine.

STAFFORD

There was a young crook called Stafford
Who bought goods he couldn't afford.
He was a compulsive spender,
And a consistent offender,
And was always trying to defraud.

STAN

A rather dotty man called Stan
Went off to have a brain scan.
The doctors were astounded
When the rays rebounded,
Which was not according to plan.

STANLEY

There was a strange man called Stanley
Whom I thought was a trifle unmanly.
He used to wear mascara
And a rather large tiara,
Which perched on his head so grandly.

STEF

There was a young sports girl called Stef
Who wanted to work as a ref.
It was a bit of a shock
When she arrived in Bangkok
To find that they expected a chef.

STEFAN

There was a young gambler called Stefan
Whose lucky number was seven.
On a certain racecourse,
He bet all on a horse.
But it came in at number eleven.

STEFANIE (ALSO STEPHANIE)

> There was a young gardener called Stefanie
> Who sat in the Garden of Gethsemane.
> With no Israelite
> Around or in sight,
> She went and stole an anemone.

STELLA

> There was a young girl called Stella,
> Who went to an old fortune-teller.
> She was told that a stranger
> Would place her in danger ,
> By giving her a spot of rubella.

STELLE

> A young beachcomber called Stelle
> Once picked up a large seashell.
> She held it to her ear
> And found nothing there –
> Or was it just one decibel?

STEPHANIE. SEE STEFANIE.

STEPHEN (ALSO STEVEN)

> There was a young coalman called Stephen
> Who got fed up with lifting and heavin'.
> He went to some markets
> To learn to make baskets,
> And was promptly told to get weavin'.

STERLING

> There was a young soldier called Sterling
> Who once met that Hermann Göring.
> He chortled with mirth
> At the size of the girth
> And the sight of "spare tyres" unfurling.

STEVE

There was a young swain called Steve
Who was inclined to be rather naïve.
When he was doing
All of his wooing,
He wore his heart on his sleeve.

STEVEN. SEE STEPHEN.

STEVIE

There was a young man called Stevie
Who owned a battered old TV.
When he was told,
"Adjust the vertical hold!"
He just got enraged and real peevy.

STU

There was a young brave called Stu
Who lived for a year with the Sioux.
He got the sack
For riding bareback,
And wearing a feather too few.

SU (ALSO SUE)

There was a vague girl called Su
Who joined an odd-looking queue.
She said, "Where does this go?
Does anyone know?"
They replied, "It's just up to you."

SUKI

There was a odd girl called Suki
Who found her hotel a bit spooky.
She decided her host
Was really a ghost,
And anyway the whole place was kookie.

SUNNY. SEE SONNIE.

SUSAN

Married to a gambler was Susan
Whose husband was always boozin'.
One day in his chowder,
She inserted a powder,
And his end was not of his choosin'.

SUSI (ALSO SUSIE, SUZI, SUZIE AND SUZY)

She was fond of a drink was our Susi
And she was always a little bit woozy.
That might be okay,
But she overdid it one day,
And she drowned in her own jacuzzi.

SUZANNA (ALSO SUZANNAH)

An enterprising girl called Suzanna
Used to copy some jokes with her scanner.
When she'd printed them out,
She got a boy scout
To sell each one for a tanner.

SUZANNE

There was a shrewd girl called Suzanne
Who thought out a wonderful plan.
She'd wear jewels and sable,
Then bet at a table,
And pick up a rich man in Cannes.

SUZI / SUZIE / SUZY. SEE SUSI.

SY

I once had a friend called Sy
Who lived in a house nearby.
He ruined my life
When he went off with my wife;
I miss him so much I could die.

SYBIL. SEE SIBYL.

SYD. SEE SID.

SYDNEY. SEE SIDNEY.

SYLVESTER. SEE SILVESTER.

SYLVIA. SEE SILVIA.

T

There was a strong man called Tex...

TABBI (ALSO TABBY)

> A reluctant girl called Tabbi
> Drove camels in Abu Dhabi.
> She didn't appreciate
> The even-toed ungulate,[134]
> And said she felt like a cabby.

TABITHA

> There was a young cave girl called Tabitha
> Who they said was just a blatherer.
> But she'd killed a mammoth
> On the tribal Sabbath,
> So they made her the chief hunter-gatherer.

TACITA (ALSO TACITAH)

> There was a young rider called Tacita
> Whose horse tried hard her to defeat her.
> What could she do
> But use instant glue,
> So the nag was unable to unseat her.

TACY

> There was a young model called Tacy
> Whom friends said was much too racy.
> If she went to a ball
> She'd wear nothing at all
> Or tiny see-through things that were lacy.

TAD

> There was a young nudist called Tad
> Who would walk around quite unclad.
> At our behest
> He put on a vest,
> Saying, "I really think you're mad."

---

[134] Even-toed ungulate: in this case, a camel.

TAFF

A short-sighted sailor called Taff
Once made a bit of a gaffe.
He told a young girl
A sail to unfurl.
She said, "I'm not a Wren, I'm a WAAF."

TAFFY

There was a young soldier called Taffy
Who thought he'd entered a café.
When he asked for smoked salmon,
And they said, "You mean gammon!"
He realised that this was the NAFFI.

TALLIE

There was a young cook called Tallie
Who worked in a cruise ship's galley.
They said her weight
And her funny shape
Was from eating too liberally.

TALLU

There was an austere girl called Tallu
Who no one wanted to woo.
If you paid her court
She'd cut you short,
Implying that you were non-U.[135]

---

[135] Non-U: Expression coined in the 1970s. U stands for upper-class and thus non-U is something to be *avoided* by someone aspiring to be upper-class.

TALLULAH

A grass-skirted girl called Tallulah
Once spent some time in the cooler.
They said her offence
Was burning incense
While dancing the hula-hula.

TAMARA

A shocked young girl called Tamara
Made a trip to the western Sahara.
She invited a Bedouin
To her tent for a gin
And he offered three camels to acquire her.

TAMMY

There was a young crooner called Tammy
Whose singing was said to be hammy.
To our great surprise,
He won a prize
And was on the list for a GRAMMY.[136]

TAMSIN

A prehistoric girl called Tamsin
Always perfumed her hair with jasmine.
Since zips were unknown
She used buttons of bone,
And wore clothes made only of lambskin.

---

[136] GRAMMY: US award by the National Academy of Recording Arts and Sciences.

TANDI (ALSO TANDY)

> A young horse rider called Tandi
> Always suffered from legs short and bandy.
> But for riding her cob
> They were just the job
> For that's where their shape came in handy

TANGERINE

> A jealous young girl – Tangerine,
> Fell in love with a handsome marine.
> But he preferred explosions
> To encouraging her emotions
> And went off with nitro-glycerine.

TANIA (ALSO TANYA, WHEN PRONOUNCED TAHN-YER)

> I was tutor to a dancer called Tania
> When she shocked me by saying, "Darn yer!
> You taught the precepts
> Of the cha cha cha steps;
> Now let's go learn the Beyzabanu."[137]
> *(pronounced Bay-ser-bahn-ya)*

TANSY

> There was a young girl called Tansy
> Who always tickled my fancy.
> If only I'd been bolder
> Or a little bit older…
> But then life is always so chancy.

TANYA. SEE TANIA.

---

[137] Beyzabanu Cha Cha Cha: a sequence dance.

TARA (ALSO TARAH)

A vague young girl called Tara
Allowed absolutely nothing to jar her.
She said some sort of mammal –
Or was it just a camel? –
Had carried her across the Sahara.

TATE

There was a young gourmet called Tate
Who kept increasing in weight.
But on the quiet
He started a diet,
And began to disintegrate.

TATUM

A misogamist girl called Tatum
Once said, "All men – I just hate 'em!
They give you champagne
Or take you to Spain,
Then issue an ultimatum!"

TAYLOR

A noisy young man called Taylor
Once used an enormous loud-hailer.
He was a little distraught
When he was taken to court,
And now he just shouts at his jailer.

TED

An absent-minded poet called Ted
Had little or no street cred.
He once wrote an ode
While crossing the road,
And beat death by just a short head.

TEDDIE (ALSO TEDDY)

A frustrating young girl was Teddie.
She always said that she'd be ready.
Despite words so sublime,
She was never on time
And I was generally there already.

TEENA (ALSO TINA)

A girl for good causes was Teena
And she received an unusual subpoena.
The idea was to stop
The latest crop
Of genetically mutated semolina.

TEMPESTA

There was an old gal called Tempesta
Who once danced with Victor Sylvester.
But it wasn't at a ball
In some music hall,
It was just that he wanted to test her.

TERESA

There was a delicate girl called Teresa
Whose boyfriend just wanted to please her.
Being a thoughtful being
He took her skiing,
But she thought the conditions would freeze her.

TERANCE (ALSO TERRENCE)

There was a young man called Terance
Who had a very strange-looking appearance.
He'd known since his teens
That the cause was the genes
Passed on from both of his parents.

TERRI (ALSO TERRIE AND TERRY)

There was a young tourist called Terri
Who boarded the Gosport ferry –
Or so she thought,
And she became distraught
When it set course for Londonderry.

TERRI (ALSO TERRIE AND TERRY)

There was a young barfly called Terri
Who liked to drink lots of perry.
He also drank port
By pint or by quart,
But drew the line at sweet sherry.

TERTIA

There was a young trekker called Tertia
Who went off on a trip to Persia.
She said she would rather
Have gone a bit farther,
But she suffered from grievous inertia.

TESS

A scattered-brained girl called Tess
Was always inclined to digress.
At the merest suggestion
Of asking a question,
She'd dissemble instead of saying, "Yes."

TESSA

There was a mind-reader called Tessa
Who was also a very good guesser.
She avoided the tedium
Of becoming a medium
By being a mother confessor.

TESSY

A history student called Tessy
Thought that wars were ever so messy.
She seemed hard to convince
That it was the Black Prince
Who took part in the battle of Crécy.

TEX

There was a strong man called Tex
Who entered a contest for pecs.
He was in suspense,
With his muscles all tense,
When he discovered the judge was his ex.

THAD

There was a young Scotsman called Thad
Who said, "Oh dear, I've been had.
I put a pound in the slot,
And look what I've got!
No chocs, just an old piece of plaid."

THEA

A brilliant young girl called Thea
Had a very unusual career.
She juggled with fire
Could play the lyre,
And wrote a pharmacopoeia.

THELMA

An energetic young child called Thelma
Exclaimed, "I want to excel, Ma!"
But on tearing her dress,
It was anyone's guess,
As to what she was going to tell Ma.

THEO

There was a trombonist called Theo
Who was one-third part of a trio.
They jazzed up Bizet
In a syncopated way,
And played *Carmen vivace con brio*.

THEOBALD

An *ab initio* pilot – Theobald,
Was looping a plane when it stalled.
He found himself in
An upside down spin.
But didn't know what it was called.

THEODORE

An RN Captain – Theodore,
Became a naval Commodore.
He achieved flag rank,
By firing a blank,
And so stopped a minor war.

THOMAS

There was a young thief called Thomas
Who said he had something on us.
With conscience clear
We followed him where
He managed to take everything from us.

THOR

A foul-mouthed man called Thor
Used to shake everyone to the core.
His remarks were profane
And caused much pain.
It was strange that they all shouted, "More!"

THETIS (ALSO THETYS)

There was a young lad called Thetis
Who said, "Do tell me what Pete is."
I said, "He's a duke."
But I got a rebuke:
"No, I meant, what the stuff in the sack on the seat is."

TIERNEY

There was a naïve girl called Tierney
Who won lots of money from Ernie.[138]
But she was diddled
By an accountant who fiddled,
But worst of all by her attorney.

TIFFANY (ALSO TIPHANI)

A young jazzy vicar called Tiffany
Just wanted to celebrate epiphany.
He [or she] managed to inspire
The local choir,
And trained them to swing an antiphony.[139]

TIFFY

A tardy young girl called Tiffy
Claimed she did everything in a jiffy.
But after lager and lime
She took quite a time;
And longer when she got more squiffy.

---

[138] Ernie: the computer that picks winning numbers for premium bonds.

[139] Antiphony: a type of church music.

TILDA

The mistress of the house called Tilda
Gave orders that were inclined to bewilder.
When I built an observatory
Instead of a conservatory,
She passed right out when I billed her.

TILLY (ALSO TILLIE)

There was a young girl called Tilly
Who was always incredibly silly.
She once tried to buy seats,
Including free sweets,
For the circus at Piccadilly.

TIM

There was a dull man called Tim
Well, you wouldn't say he was dim –
This might be inferred
If you use the wrong word,
But I can't find the right synonym.

TIMMY

There was a young dancer called Timmy
Who often did things on a whimmy.
He was teaching a number
Based on the rumba,
When he invented a new type of shimmy.

TIMON

A young boy from Athens called Timon
Had toys that were prone to get grime on.
His parents were bemused
But to keep him amused,
They bought him a frame to climb on.

TINA. SEE TEENA.

TINY

There was an old swimmer called Tiny
Whose pate was always so shiny.
He hadn't a clue
As to what it was due,
But it might be the salt in the briny.

TIPHANY. SEE TIFFANY.

TITUS

I was once with a geologist called Titus
When we turned over some curious detritus.
Then out jumped an adder
Getting madder and madder,
And calmly proceeded to bite us.

TOBIAS

There was an academic called Tobias
Who viewed the world with no bias.
He could reach a decision
With single-minded vision;
For he had only one eye and was pious.

TOBY

There was an aged man called Toby
Who most people thought an old fogey.
But he proved them wrong
When he put on a sarong,
And went for a stroll in the Gobi.

TOD (ALSO TODD)

There was a young corporal called Tod
Who was put in charge of a squad.
It decided to spurn
His order, "Right turn!"
And they finished up in the quod.

TOM

Said a soldier from Oz called Tom,
While checking a defective bomb,
"I feel a bit sick,
Now it's started to tick,
I'll leave it for a whinging Pom."

TOMMIE (ALSO TOMMY)

There was a young waiter called Tommie
Who obtained a job as a commis.
He had plenty of work
And the occasional perk
Due to his candid bonhomie.

TONE

There was a young man called Tone –
A master of the saxophone.
His fine syncopation
Astonished the nation,
Plus a few in the Euro zone.

TONI (ALSO TONY)

There was an old man called Toni
Whose head was thick and bony.
He said that radio
Started in Ontario,
And had never heard of Marconi.

TONIA

I once knew a girl called Tonia
Who suffered from a bout of pneumonia.
She retired to her bed
But was later found dead
When she mistakenly drank some ammonia.

TONY. SEE TONI.

TOPSIE (ALSO TOPSY)

There was a sick girl called Topsie
Who was called to the doc for a biopsy.
When she asked him why
He said in reply,
"It's better than having an autopsy."

TORQUIL

A wise young philosopher called Torquil
Said that wars solve nothing, but talk will.
He went on to say
In his curious way,
That sloth doesn't help man, but a walk will.

TOTTIE

There was an odd girl called Tottie
Who some might think was just potty.
But perhaps it is better
To change the first letter,
For really she was just slightly dotty.

TRACE

There was a pretty girl called Trace
Who we loved for her bearing and grace.
I was thinking of this
When I snatched a kiss,
But she gave me a slap on the face.

Tracie (also Tracy)

There was a young poet called Tracie
Who was known to be ever so racy.
Unlike those of John Fay,
His [or her] rhymes were risqué,
Mentioning things brief and quite lacy.

Tre

There was a young Indian called Tre
Who could only just count up to three.
He once got to four
And tried for one more
But couldn't do so in Pawnee.

Trelawny

There was a slim man called Trelawny
Who was inclined to be rather scrawny.
I could eat my hat
When his diet changed that ,
For he ate nothing but mulligatawny.[140]

Tremaine

There was a young artist – Tremaine,
Who tried to forge "The Hay Wain".[141]
He sat on a tussock
In a place down in Suffolk
But the pond had gone down the drain.

---

[140] Mulligatawny: a highly seasoned soup, originally from India.
[141] "The Hay Wain": a painting by John Constable.

TREVOR

There was a young man called Trevor
Who was handsome and brave and clever.
I have no cause
To mention his flaws,
They are of no importance whatsoever.

TRICIA (ALSO TRISHA)

A very thin girl called Tricia
Once enlisted in the local militia.
By the San Andreas fault,
The sergeant yelled, "Halt!"
And she disappeared right down a fissure.

TRIS

There was a young man called Tris
Who once went out with a miss.
He sang her a song
But went on too long,
And missed out on the ultimate bliss.

TRISTAM

A young skeet shooter called Tristam,
Would take aim but invariably missed 'em.
He got frustrated,
As can be related,
And blamed it all on the system.

TRISTAN

A car enthusiast called Tristan
Had a fist that resembled a piston.
His upper limb was odd,
Just like an old con-rod,
And a sump was used to rest his wrist on.

TRISH

A highland girl called Trish
Was proud of being Scottish.
She wore a dirk,
Plus a wry sort of smirk,
And was inclined to be standoffish.

TRISHA. SEE TRICIA.

TRIXIE

A Maryland woman called Trixie
Once knew both Mason and Dixie.
She said the latter looked fine
When drawing a line,
But Mason resembled a pixie.

TROY

There was a young sailor called Troy
Who once shouted out, "Ship ahoy!"
He got very irate
When the reply came late,
And they explained, "We were just being coy."

TRUDE (PRONOUNCED TRUDAH)

There was a vociferous girl called Trude
Who just got shrewder and shrewder.
At any sort of do
She'd force her point of view.
In the end we had to exclude her.

TRUDI (ALSO TRUDIE AND TRUDY)

A motherly young girl called Trudi
Was inclined to be somewhat moody.
Some days it would seem
That she was in a dream,
And in others she looked quite broody.

TUDOR

There was a young angler called Tudor
Who once caught a large barracuda.
He stuffed it full
Of old cotton wool
And used it as a draught excluder.

TYRONE

There was a young man called Tyrone
Who would never go to the phone.
He used his retriever
To pick up the receiver,
Then toss it a very small bone.

TYRUS

I once had a boss called Tyrus
Who held certain things were desirous:
"Comfortable seating,
But no central heating,
And memos written on papyrus."

There was a young pianist — Umberto…

UDALL

There was an old man called Udall
Whose outlook was distinctly feudal.
He'd call you a serf
And make you cut turf,
And refer to you as his poodle.

UDELLA

There was a young actress – Udella,
Who had the part of Cinderella.
She suffered a reversal
During the dress rehearsal
When she tripped on a stage umbrella.

UDELLE

A bit of a flirt was Udelle
But was quite unable to spell.
She'd confuse the Bs
With Ts and Ps –
But other things she did really well.

UDOLF

There was a sportsman named Udolf
Which looks like a misprint for Rudolf.
He spent all his time
Seeking errors in rhyme,
Or perfecting putting at golf.

ULYSSES

There was a landlord called Ulysses
Who said, "Look 'ere, all yew lessees:
If yew don't shut the door,
The whole of that floor
Gets a draught and all of us freezes."

UMBERTO

There was a young pianist – Umberto,
Who could play Grieg's Piano Concerto.
And just for kicks
He'll do Chopsticks,
Performed with his little bare toe.

UNA

A fastidious girl called Una
Once met a young Induna.[142]
But she said good-bye
When he used his assegai
As a fork to eat up his tuna.

UNDINE

A young native girl called Undine
Was revered as an African Sun Queen.
But it seems a bit strange
That she had to arrange
For a delivery of special sunscreen.

UNICE. SEE EUNICE.

UNITY

A fast young girl called Unity
Had diplomatic immunity.
She used CD plates
As a ploy for getting dates,
And used it at every opportunity.

---

[142] Induna: Zulu military chief.

UNWIN

A brash Highland lad called Unwin
Used to make such a thundering din.
He went to Glen Bogle
Where he learnt to yodel –
Now they're seeking his next of kin…

URBAN

There was an old toper called Urban
Whose outlook was somewhat suburban.
He thought it a sin
To drink neat gin,
And preferred his drink to be bourbon.

URI

There was a young man called Uri
Who was charged with dating a houri.
He said in his defence
That he'd paid her ten cents
For showing him the way to Missouri.

URIAH

A confidence trickster called Uriah
Used to claim he was the new Messiah.
To my recollection,
He took a collection,
And then did a rather brisk flyer.

URSE

There was a young student called Urse
Who thought Irish was somewhat diverse.
She tried to decrypt
The Ogham script,[143]
But found the text a bit terse.

---

[143] Ogham script: a 4th century inscription in Erse.

Ursie

There was a friendly girl called Ursie
Who was offered a drink by Circe.[144]
She felt it was infra dig[145]
To be turned into a pig,
But that sorceress showed her no mercy.

Ursula

A bit of a flirt was young Ursula
And her embraces were distinctly muscular.
She said that a kiss
Was the ultimate bliss,
So her pleasures were entirely oscular.

---

[144] Circe: an enchantress who transformed all who drank of her cup into swine.

[145] Infra dig: beneath one's dignity; unbecoming.

V

There was a young tourist called Vera…

VADIM

A would-be actor called Vadim
Couldn't start 'cos his father forbade him.
He thought it wise
To put on a disguise,
But Pa just said, "Why, that's 'im!"

VAL

There was an old man called Val
Who fought in Guadalcanal.
He said that the Japs
Were terrible chaps,
Not the sort he'd like as a pal.

VALENTINE

There was an old man – Valentine,
Who met up with Eisenstein.[146]
The latter did tempt him
To help with *Potemkin,*
But that honour he had to decline.

VALENTINO

A betting man called Valentino
Was told to study the neutrino.
He felt such an ass
Scanning bits with no mass,
That he went off to play the casino.

VALERIA

There was a garden-girl called Valeria
Who suffered from mild hysteria.
This was especially so
When there was no show
Of flowers on her little wisteria.

---

[146] Eisenstein: Russian film director. He made the famous film *The Battleship Potemkin* in 1925.

VALERIE (ALSO VALERY)

I was to model for a painter called Valerie
So I counted so carefully each calorie.
I just couldn't wait
To reduce my weight
For I would be hung in the National Gallery.

VALIANT

Said a sore old gardener called Valiant,
"How do I kill that bally ant.
I know it's quite rare
To be bitten right here.
Have I caught the darned thing? No I haven't."

VAN

There was a young Portuguese called Van
Who used to be an also-ran.
He then took up judo,
Which cost one escudo,
And now he's a brilliant tenth dan.

VANCE

A lovelorn young man called Vance
Just wanted to find romance.
He thought it wise
To advertise,
But couldn't afford the finance.

VANESSA (ALSO VENESSA)

There was a computer girl called Vanessa
Who had trouble with her word processor.
She was somewhat abashed
When her machine crashed,
And up shot her normal blood pressure.

VANNY

A young witch of a girl called Vanny
Had powers that were usually uncanny.
But when she said the moon
Would turn blue in June,
I'd rather believe my granny.

VAUGHAN (ALSO VAUGHN)

There was a young man called Vaughan
Who had neither brains nor brawn.
He once wrote an ode
In a sort of Morse code,
And was seen by two doctors next morn.

VENESSA. SEE VANESSA.

VENETIA

A gardening girl called Venetia
Specialised in growing aubretia.
Her local adviser
Said, "Use fertiliser
Made of peat and milk of magnesia."

VENN

There was a young soldier called Venn
Who said he had at last heard the gen.[147]
"The enemy's advancing –
Or is Emmy going dancing?
Perhaps you could say that again."

---

[147] Gen: information.

VERA

There was a young tourist called Vera
Who went to the sunny Riviera.
She didn't like that,
So she came right back –
Just as well, 'cos the French couldn't bear her.

VERGIL (ALSO VIRGIL)

A young entrepreneur called Vergil
Said, "Nothing will depress like a dirge will.
But in business, it's true
That out of the blue,
Nothing can succeed like a merge will."

VERITY

There was a young manager called Verity
Who was subject to bouts of asperity.
She'd say she was boss,
Which made me quite cross;
I wonder she had the temerity.

VERNA

A naïve young girl called Verna
Said chemistry just didn't concern her.
She became an importer
Of dehydrated water,
And found she had a nice little earner.

VERNON

There was a young sailor called Vernon
Who backed his boat in stern on.
He offered a prayer
But his rudder hit the pier.
And then he had nothing to turn on.

VERONA

A foolish young girl called Verona
Once ran with the bulls in Pamplona.
She said to one steer,
"Come, come, never fear!"
But the bull made her a blood donor.

VERONICA

There was an old lady called Veronica
Who won a prize for her japonica.
She told me not to tell
How she did so well,
"I play to it on my harmonica!"

VÉRONIQUE

There was a weird girl – Véronique,
Who, one might say, was unique.
Others not so kind
Thought her a bind,
While some said she was just a freak.

VESTA

There was a gifted girl called Vesta
Who was known as a bit of a jester.
She'd play Gershwin
In the style of Joplin,
And syncopate on her celesta.

VI

A serious young student called Vi
Asked me, "What's this little word 'Xi'?"
I said, "Oh, gee,
It's Greek to me!"
But she didn't see the wink in my eye.

VIC (ALSO VICK)

There was an old crook called Vic
Who had just escaped from the nick.
Being tall,
He just climbed a wall,
Then made a hole with a stick.

VICCI (ALSO VICCY AND VIKKI)

A thoughtful young girl called Vicci
Said that life could be a bit tricky,
"If you drop a jammy bun
The chances are four to one
That the side on the floor will be sticky."

VICKY

There was a fat man called Vicky
Who said that health can be tricky.
"I'm the one
Who weighs half a ton
And my poor old ticker is dicky."

VICTOR

A man from Brazil called Victor
Was confused by laws and dicta.[148]
He read with amazement
The rules of engagement
For fighting a boa constrictor.

VICTORIA

Said a fanciful girl called Victoria
"I'm suffering from phantasmagoria.
I see men in my dreams
Passing by me in teams,
I'm in a permanent state of euphoria."

---

[148] Dicta: plural of dictum.

VIDA

An atomic scientist called Vida
Was, as a mother, a world leader.
After two pairs of twins,
She gave birth to quins,
And became known as a very fast breeder.

VIKKY. SEE VICCI.

VINCE

There was a young man called Vince
Who was great at dropping hints.
But when I heard him say
Hot pants were passé,
I've ignored him ever since.

VINCENT

There was an old lag called Vincent
Who liked the gifts his kin sent.
They added a refinement
To his enforced confinement,
But he always said, "I'm innocent."

VINNY

An athletic young girl called Vinny
Would do strange things for a guinea.
She once swam the Channel
Wrapped up in a flannel,
With her food tied up in her pinny.

VIOLA

There was a rash gambler – Viola
Who got tight on a glass of my Cola.
She then bet a ton
At odds: ten to one.
But she always was a high roller.

VIOLET

There was a young girl called Violet
Who invented a new type of eyelet.
She went to Arkansas
To check on the law
And to make her patent inviolate.

VIOLETTA

There was a young girl – Violetta,
Who once wrote a nasty vile letter.
She did it again
With her poison pen
Until they managed to get her.

VIRGIL. SEE VERGIL.

VIRGINIA

There was a slim girl called Virginia
Whose dimensions were mostly linear.
Don't get me wrong,
But when she wore a sarong,
The other parameters were mini-er.

VITA

There was a careless girl called Vita
Who upset the electric heater.
It was a matter of arbitration
In the resulting conflagration
Whether she or her sister were fleeter.

VIV (ALSO VYV)

There was a an old lady called Viv
Who went to a well with a sieve.
Her resulting frustration
Amused the whole nation,
And her fan mail was most impressive.

VIVIAN (ALSO VYVIAN [F], VIVIEN [F & M], AND VIVIENNE [F])

There was a young girl [boy] called Vivian
Who thought that her [his] forbears were amphibian.
But I told her [him] straight
That it was decreed by fate,
That they were, in fact, just simian.

VIVIE

There was a leading Wren called Vivie
Who was demobbed and was once more a civvy.
She never would speak
Of her time in the fleet,
For there were secrets to which she was privy.

VIVIEN / VIVIENNE. SEE VIVIAN.

VIVIETTE

There was a another Wren called Viviette
Who stayed on, so was not a civvy yet.
She started investing,
Which she found interesting,
But said that she had had no divvy yet.

VONNIE

There was a pretty girl called Vonnie
Who everyone thought so bonny.
She had a body like Venus –
Or similar genus –
And a neck curvaceous and swanny.

VYV. SEE VIV.

VYVIAN. SEE VIVIAN.

W

Our schoolie is a man named Waldo...

WALDO

Our schoolie is a man named Waldo
And as a fine teacher he's all go.
Any hair on his pate
Is hard to locate,
So that's why we call him Old Baldo.

WALLACE

A young gardening girl called Wallace
Is desperately in need of some solace.
The lack of rain,
And then a hurricane,
Have killed her genetically modified orris.[149]

WALT

There was a young gymnast called Walt
Who had good reason to exalt.
After trying for a day,
He was able to say,
He could perform a back somersault.

WALTER

There was a young choirboy called Walter
Who was accused of stealing a psalter.
But before he could plead
He had to be freed,
For it was found under a hat on the altar.

WANDA

A radio expert called Wanda
Once built a home-made transponder.
It didn't do quite
What she thought it might,
And teleported her way out yonder.

---

[149] Orris: a species of iris.

WARREN

A newly arrived man called Warren
Was accused of being too foreign.
When he wore the wrong tartan
In the town of Dumbarton,
They found a microdot under his sporran.

WAT (ALSO WATT)

There was a young dancer called Wat
Who could do a graceful gavotte.
He didn't choose
To do the blues
And jazzed up the slow foxtrot.

WAIN (ALSO WAYNE)

An old hypochondriac called Wain
Had an outlook less than urbane.
But he started to panic
And got quite manic
When he developed a large chilblain.

WEND

There was a furious author called Wend
Who published an article she'd penned.
She complained that the editor
Tried to discredit her,
And her copyright she had to defend.

WENDELL

There was an old gardener called Wendell
Who came from a district near Kendall.
Many cried "Oh!"
At the Chelsea Flower Show
When he showed them his daff with a tendril.

WENDY

A fresh young girl called Wendy
Had an outlook both modern and trendy.
I liked the old days,
She preferred the new ways,
But she was always there to defend me.

WES

An Egyptian dragoman called Wes
Always goes out in a fez.
When he shows me the Sphinx,
I can't tell what he thinks,
Nor can I grasp what he says.

WESLA

There was a tough girl called Wesla
Who trained as a female wrestler.
They asked the local priest
To discourage her at least,
But all he could do was to bless her.

WILF

There was a young gardener called Wilf
Who wanted to make a fine tilth.
Using the rake
Was a "piece of cake",
But he got all covered with filth.

WILFRED

There was a young gardener called Wilfred
Who they say always planned to kill Fred.
He was using a rake
And pierced a vein by mistake;
But he didn't intend it – so Bill said.

WILFREDA

There was a sick girl called Wilfreda
Whose doc's idea was to bleed her.
As she lay dying,
The doc said, "I'm trying,
But I really hope you don't need her."

WILHELMINA

There was a young tot – Wilhelmina,
Whose ma did her best to wean her.
She failed with coffee
And sticky toffee,
But had success with cold semolina.

WILKIE

There was an old rep called Wilkie
Whose hands were all pappy and silky.
He was suave and urbane,
Sold me a time-share in Spain,
And I'm sure he intended to bilk me.

WILL

A very small boy called Will
Once ran up an enormous bill.
He came to a stop
Below the top,
'Cos the pelican wouldn't keep still.

WILLA

There was a young author called Willa
Who wrote a sordid crime thriller.
Some said the plot
Was good – others not;
But no one detected the killer.

WILLIAM

Said a young little boy called William,
"If you think me a fool – well I am.
It would be no strain
To weigh my brain
For it'll come to just one milligram."

WILLIE (ALSO WILLY)

There was a greedy old man called Willie
Who refused to eat piccalilli.
He'd eat some greens,
Such as fresh runner beans,
Or cream cakes smothered in chilli.

WILLOUGHBY

There was a young author called Willoughby
Who wrote a successful trilogy.
At least, it would've been
If he hadn't come clean
And admitted he'd copied Phil Dillowby.

WILLOW

An animal-loving girl called Willow
Once slept with her pet armadillo.
She found it frustrating
When its armour plating
Was there instead of her pillow.

WILLY. SEE WILLIE.

WILMOT

There was an old man called Wilmot
A Chief Petty Officer, that's what.
He went to sea
Got an MBE,
Then was put in charge at Gospot.[150]

WIN (ALSO WYNN AND WYNNE)

Said a strong-minded girl called Win,
"I always wear a strong hat pin.
I certainly reckon
It's a useful weapon;
It's legal and penetrates skin!"

WINDSOR

A cheese-paring man called Windsor
Once bought an old-fashioned mincer.
It was covered in dirt,
And just would not work,
And he told me, "I just cannot win, sir."

WINIFRED

A pretty young girl – Winifred,
Once went for a cruise in the Med.
But after the spree
On the Isle of Capri,
She went a little bit soft in the head.

WINNA

There was a stout girl called Winna,
Who declared she ought to be thinner.
She worked out a diet
And said that she'd try it,
But not till she'd had Christmas dinner.

---

[150] Gospot: poetic licence for Gosport.

WINNIE

> An impecunious man called Winnie
> Went and bought a second-hand Mini.
> He found its top speed
> Was very slow indeed.
> But what do you expect for one guinea?

WINNIE

> There was an "It" girl called Winnie
> Who thought she looked too skinny.
> But most men felt
> That she looked very svelte,
> And loved her see-through pinny.

WOODROW

> There was a young nudist – Woodrow,
> Who went where no man dared go.
> He walked from Nairobi
> To the edge of the Gobi
> Wearing only a bright dickey bow.

WOODY

> There was a strange man called Woody
> And most people said, "Oh, how could he?"
> But an opposing view
> Was taken by a few,
> Who said, "Did he do that? Oh goody!"

WYATT

> There was a young rebel called Wyatt
> Who tried to incite a riot.
> When things went wrong,
> He went to Hong Kong
> And slipped away on the quiet.

WYNN / WYNNE. SEE WIN.

A fortune-teller called Xanthe…

XANTHE

A fortune-teller called Xanthe
Was an expert in chiromancy.
She'd exercise charm
When she looked at your palm,
Then say what she thought you'd fancy.

XENA

A young foreign girl called Xena
Was trained as a ballerina.
But it was a limited vocation
For her exotic location,
Was on the island of St Helena.

XANTHUS

There was an old man called Xanthus
Who had an unusual canthus.[151]
It gave his face
The special grace
To look like a pink dianthus.[152]

XAVIER

An angry Sicilian called Xavier
Once failed a test for the mafia.
But he was told it was twaddle
To stick pins in a model
Of a godfather made up of raffia.[153]

---

[151] Canthus: the angle at which the upper and lower eyelids meet.

[152] Dianthus: a flowering plant.

[153] Raffia: a soft fibre used for making hats, baskets, mats, etc.

XENOS

A studious old Greek called Xenos
Was worried about his pen loss.
He went to write a scroll
About something droll,
But discovered he'd left it in Lemnos.

XERXES

There was an old king called Xerxes
Who ordered, "Get down on your knees!
You men must kow-tow,
Or at least give a bow –
I'm not one for 'Do as you please'!"

Y

There was a strange man called Yancy...

Yaffa

A bad-mannered girl called Yaffa
Once tried for a job as a gaffer.
But because of the fact
That she had no tact,
Not one of the firms would have her.

Yance

A flabby young man called Yance
Once went for a run around Hants.
He felt like death,
And as for his breath –
Like him, it came in short pants.

Yancy

There was a strange man called Yancy
Whose chosen career was chancy.
The fire brigade
Thought him a renegade
For he'd previously tried pyromancy.[154]

Yas

There was a young deb called Yas
Who implored me to take her to Das.
But it had no style
This "paradise" isle;
It was oil wells and machinery en masse.

---

[154] Pyromancy: prophecy by fire.

YASMINE

There was a graceful girl called Yasmine
Whom some said was just a has-been.
But I was entranced
By the way she danced –
Especially the Foxtrot Jasmine.[155]

YATES

There was a fine man called Yates
Who lived in a house with no gates.
He said this was so
Folk could come and go
Without having any long waits.

YEDDA

An inventive young girl called Yedda
Once bought a new garden shredder.
She put in some milk
Plus stuff of that ilk,
Switched on and found she'd made cheddar.

YEOMAN

Said an army recruit called Yeoman,
"I considered my name was an omen,
But they make me a sarge
And they put me in charge
Of getting rid of that snowman."

YETTA

An obnoxious old woman called Yetta
Said that someone was out to get her.
So I contacted a few
Of a mafia crew,
And said they could borrow my biretta.

---

[155] Jasmine Foxtrot: a sequence dance.

YNEZ

An old millionairess called Ynez
Was looking for the best des res.
She found a castle in Spain
But lost it again
To a man in a little green fez.

YOLA

There was a new Wren called Yola
Who seemed to need a condoler.
She'd just played a game,
And had lost just the same,
It was like Bingo, but called Tombola.

YOLANDA

There was a strong girl called Yolanda
Who met an aggressive giant panda.
There were a series of hugs
And some frenzied tugs.
She won, but the keepers then banned her.

YORICK

There was a young man called Yorick
A guy we think as symbolic.
It must be dull
To be out of one's skull,
But perhaps he was an alcoholic.

YULES

A forward young man called Yules
Was inclined to ignore all the rules.
He would often declare
For all to hear
That rules were just made for fools.

YVETTE

There was a young blonde called Yvette
Who wanted to marry a vet.
But he didn't care
For the shade of her hair,
Or the fact that she wore flannelette.

YVONA

There was a young girl called Yvona
Who was a bit of a loner.
Like the lady above,
She never found love –
But perhaps one day I'll phone her.

Z

A rather lame man called Zac...

ZAC (ALSO ZACK)

A rather lame man called Zac
Went off to visit the quack.
"So," said that burke,
"Your knee won't work!
I'll dress it then give it a whack."

ZACHARIAH

There was a bad man – Zachariah,
Who took a trip in a Black Maria.[156]
Perhaps I should mention
That wasn't his intention,
And it wasn't 'cos he sang in the choir.

ZANE

There was a young rider called Zane
Whose horse got stuck in the Seine.
Using a lasso
And some superglue
He pulled it out by its mane.

ZAHRA (ALSO ZARA)

There was a young girl called Zahra
Who found nightclubs tried to bar her.
They said bringing animals
Was okay for cannibals,
But not, please, an old capybara.[157]

---

[156] Black Maria: a police vehicle for transporting criminals.

[157] Capybara: a rodent, native of South America resembling a large guinea pig.

ZEB

I once had a lodger called Zeb
Who complained he was underfed.
He weighed twenty stone
So I was tired of his moans,
His accusations made me see red.

ZEBEDEE

An itchy young man – Zebedee,
Said he had a flea on his knee.
He'd thought it out
While drinking a stout –
That the guilty party was me!

ZEKE

There was a keen student called Zeke
Who said he'd like to learn Greek.
He didn't like the grammar,
But got as far as gamma –
And that took most of the week.

ZELDA

A factory girl called Zelda
Was learning to become a welder.
She thought it obscene
To use oxyacetylene,
And wouldn't believe "wot oi telled 'er".

ZELMA

An Amazon fighter called Zelma
Defied anyone to unhelm her.
Then along came Hugh
With a fresh Irish stew,
And the smell did overwhelm her.

ZENA

There was a young sailor called Zena
Who was an expert trampoliner.
She could do a somersault
Without a single fault
While anchored in the marina.

ZENNA

A protected young girl called Zenna
Was guarded by a vigilant duenna.
One day she got free
And went on the spree,
Returning with her hair dyed with henna.

ZENO

An atomic scientist called Zeno
Once found a brand-new neutrino.
When that had gone,
He split a proton,
But found that one half was albino.

ZEPH

A rather crude man called Zeph
Said that he'd read Macbeth.
He thought the three witches
Were rotten bitches
To have a part in Duncan's death.

ZETTA

An Italian girl called Zetta
Once knitted a bright red sweater.
It glowed in the dark
And lit the spark
For a dreadful Sicilian vendetta.

ZEUS

There was an old god called Zeus
Who felt he wasn't much use.
But he made many laws
Behind closed doors
Before he played fast and loose.

ZIA

An untidy girl called Zia
Said she had nothing to wear.
But she wouldn't deposit
Her clothes in the closet
So could never find quite the right gear.

ZIAN

There was a young golfer called Zian
Who couldn't believe what he was seein'.
A hundred yards from the pin,
And with a sheepish grin,
A player just lifted his ball and was teein'.

ZINNIA

An inquisitive child called Zinnia
Once asked me which was grinnier:
A Cheshire cat
A well-fed gnat,
Or something rectilinear.

ZITA

There was a young barmaid called Zita
Who sold Cointreau by the litre.
To make quite sure
She didn't give more,
She measured it out with a meter.

ZIVA

A lazy young girl called Ziva
Was rated as an under-achiever.
She was never in a hurry
And didn't seem to worry,
And nothing I said would peeve her.

ZOË

A young nanny from Oz called Zoë
Decided she'd nurse a joey.
But it tended to slouch
And stay in its pouch;
It certainly was not very go-ey.

ZOLA

There was a young explorer called Zola
Whose expeditions were polar.
She started off skint,
But made quite a mint
When she found an iceberg of Cola.

ZONA

A girl from Norway called Zona
Bought a brand new bottle of toner.
She also bought a doll
Dressed just like a troll,
All for the price of one krone.

ZORA

A long-nosed girl called Zora
Went in for a prize as a snorer.
The others' intonations
Couldn't match her detonations,
And she was by far the top scorer.

ZSA

A boastful young girl called Zsa
Told me she'd met the young Shah.
I tried not to upset her,
But when I went one better,
She just looked at me and cried, "Bah!"

ZSA-ZSA

There was a young girl called Zsa-Zsa
Who could do a fantastic cha cha.
And during that dance
If she gave you a glance
It would send most all of us gaga.

Printed in the United Kingdom
by Lightning Source UK Ltd.
103256UKS00001B/1-30